AUTHENTIC TRANSCRIPTIONS
WITH NOTES AND TABLATURE

P9-CRT-025

THE CREAM OF
CLAPTON

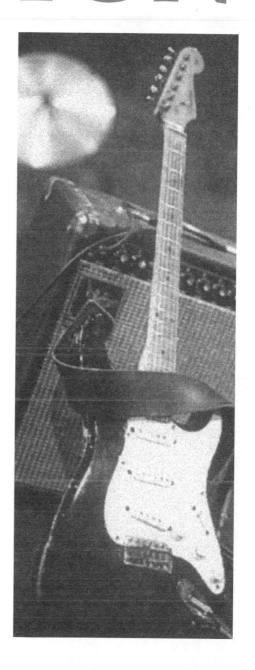

ISBN 0-7935-5151-x

HAL•LEONARD™

THE CREAM OF
CLAPTON

ODYSSEY OF A GUITAR PLAYER

by Dave Rubin

Though he was briefly called "Slowhand" in the Yardbirds, Eric Clapton has never needed a nickname. Chet Atkins was once called "Mr. Guitar," but his name alone bespeaks country guitar just as Clapton's does rock guitar. With the blues as his constant companion, he has gone from mod London to sunny Miami, from intense, private woodshedding on the electric guitar to the public display of his acoustic chops on MTV.

Eric Patrick Clapton was born in Ripley, England on March 30, 1945. Hearing an album by Big Bill Broonzy as a young teen inspired him to acquire an acoustic guitar. By age 15 he was discouraged, however, and quit practicing while deciding to pursue a career as a stained glass designer after finishing secondary school. Two years later he was asked to terminate his enrollment at the Kingston School for Art after only two months of study. A passion for the history of blues and R&B was coinciding with a renewed interest in playing the guitar. Though his first idols were Chuck Berry and Bo Diddley, he was drawn back to Big Bill (who was popular in England during the '50s) and, through him, to Robert Johnson, Blind Boy Fuller, Son House, Skip James and Blind Lemon Jefferson.

Flush with some proficiency, Clapton formed the Roosters with future Rolling Stone Brian Jones and future Manfred Mann-ers Tom McGuiness and Paul Jones. Within two months the Roosters were history and Clapton was with Casey Jones and the Engineers, a Mersey beat band from Liverpool. In a move that would become a pattern throughout his career, he left the pop group after two weeks due to his purist sensibilities. Meanwhile, the Rolling Stones, with ex-Rooster Brian Jones, had out grown their local gig at the Crawdaddy Club in Richmond by 1963, leaving a void for the up and coming Yardbirds to fill. Taking over for their former lead guitarist Top Topham, Clapton added authentic blues credibility to a pre-psychedelic band that would eventually merge pop, rock, folk, Indian, Mid-Eastern and blues influences on Jeff Beck's watch, with the odd Gregorian Chant tossed in for experimental purposes. Though he got to flash his hard won blues licks on Chicago-style numbers like "I Ain't Got You" and "Got To Hurry," singer Keith Relf had his eye on the prize, and Clapton was gone after eighteen months in 1965, just as the band was hitting the charts with "For Your Love."

With his reputation growing among London's underground blues community, the patriarchal John Mayall tapped Clapton for his Bluesbreakers. After eighteen months of burning brightly, even while chafing under Mayall's rigid orthodoxy, he emerged restless and a reluctant guitar hero, inspiring the infamous "Clapton Is God" graffiti that would come to haunt him. This time he wanted something more popular and contemporary.

In June 1966 a casual event occurred that would shift the rock world on its axis. Drummer Ginger Baker sat in with the Bluesbreakers joining the recently hired bassist Jack Bruce in the rhythm section. Clapton had an epiphany and asked Bruce and Baker to follow him in forming a blues-rock power trio called Cream. When *Fresh Cream* was released six months later in December, everyone on both sides of the Atlantic was finally hearing what would become one of rock's most enduring instrumental voices.

The Cream of Clapton documents this phenomenon from Cream's "I Feel Free" to "I Can't Stand It" from Clapton's *Another Ticket* (1981). Every song tells a story from the Eric Clapton saga.

1. "I Feel Free" (1966): the opening cut from the debut album expresses the collective mood of the band. Jack Bruce sings his modal composition while Clapton plays a short, sustained solo mimicking the melody.

2. "The Sunshine of Your Love" (1967): Bruce's classic with the blues changes and the immortal bass line hook. Clapton quotes "Blue Moon" with a flute-like tone in his solo.

3. "White Room" (1968): a dramatic Bruce anthem with Clapton's wah-wha forging a new sound into rock's consciousness.

4. "Crossroads (Cross Road Blues)" (1968): from the epochal *Wheels of Fire* album. This live track finds Clapton singing Robert Johnson's Delta blues classic and playing like a strange being from another planet. Still the standard for blues-rockers to measure themselves against … just ask Van Halen.

5. "Badge" (1969): from Cream's swan song, "Goodbye Cream." Alas, they only held it together for two years. Clapton co-wrote this classic with George Harrison (who played rhythm guitar on the recording) and belted out a most memorable, melodic, major scale solo.

6. "Presence of the Lord" (1969): from the superhyped but doomed supergroup, Blind Faith, featuring Stevie Winwood and Ginger Baker. Clapton found religion and his voice, but he lost the band due to ego clashes.

7. "Blues Power" (1970): rock, not blues, from the long anticipated Eric Clapton solo album. Produced by Delaney Bramlett, whom he had been touring with in a sideman capacity since the breakup of Blind Faith. Clapton is writing and singing like a laid back Southern rocker, while laying down his big fat Gibsons for a rather thin-sounding Strat.

8. "After Midnight" (1970): his first J.J. Cale cover, and a minor hit. Harder rocking than the self penned "Blues Power", with gospel-style backing vocals and a deliberately non-virtuosic solo.

9. "Let It Rain" (1970): another original composition from the solo album that sounds like a warm up for "Layla." The core musicians would go on to become Derek and the Dominoes.

10. "Bell Bottom Blues" (1970): From Clapton's monumental Derek and the Dominoes album, *Layla and Other Assorted Love Songs*. Definitely not a blues, but an anguished plea in the form of a touching rock ballad. Duane Allman's towering presence invigorates and challenges Clapton throughout the album, particularly on the epic blues jams.

11. "Layla" (1970): considered by many to be Clapton's crowning achievement, and an albatross around his neck ever since. Allman wrote the intro hook and played stratospheric slide. Written for Patti Harrison, George's wife, with whom Clapton was involved.

12. "I Shot the Sheriff" (1974): MOR Reggae from the Bob Marley catalog. A hit single from *461 Ocean Boulevard* (recorded in Miami, Florida). Clapton's comeback album after a near tragic period of substance abuse.

13. "Let It Grow" (1974): Clapton's pop side in all its glory (?) from *461 Ocean Boulevard*.

14. "Knocking On Heaven's Door" (1975): a Reggae version of Dylan's movie tune from *Pat Garrett and Billy the Kid*. Soulful singing and a rare slide solo as Clapton takes on the appearance of an American cowboy.

15. "Hello Old Friend" (1976): Clapton pays a musical tribute to old friend George Harrison with a tune and a slide lick that could have come from the former Beatle's "All Things Must Pass."

16. "Cocaine" (1977): from Clapton's highly-touted "comeback" album *Slowhand* and the talented pen of J.J. Cale. Clapton shows tantalizing glimpses of his old fiery self and the song becomes a concert favorite.

17. "Wonderful Tonight" (1977): the pop hit from *Slowhand*. Though saccharine and sentimental, it shows Clapton's ability to write and play appealing melodies. Written for then-wife, Patti Boyd Harrison Clapton.

18. "Promises" (1978): Clapton displays his burnished vocal chops on this bouncy folk-rocker. The slide is again present as a melodic voice.

19. "I Can't Stand It" (1981): a tentative rocker from the early '80s. The great Albert Lee takes the Duane Allman role in providing a foil for Clapton on *Another Ticket*, the album from which this cut was lifted.

I Feel Free

Words and Music by Jack Bruce and Pete Brown

* Background vocals 2nd time only.

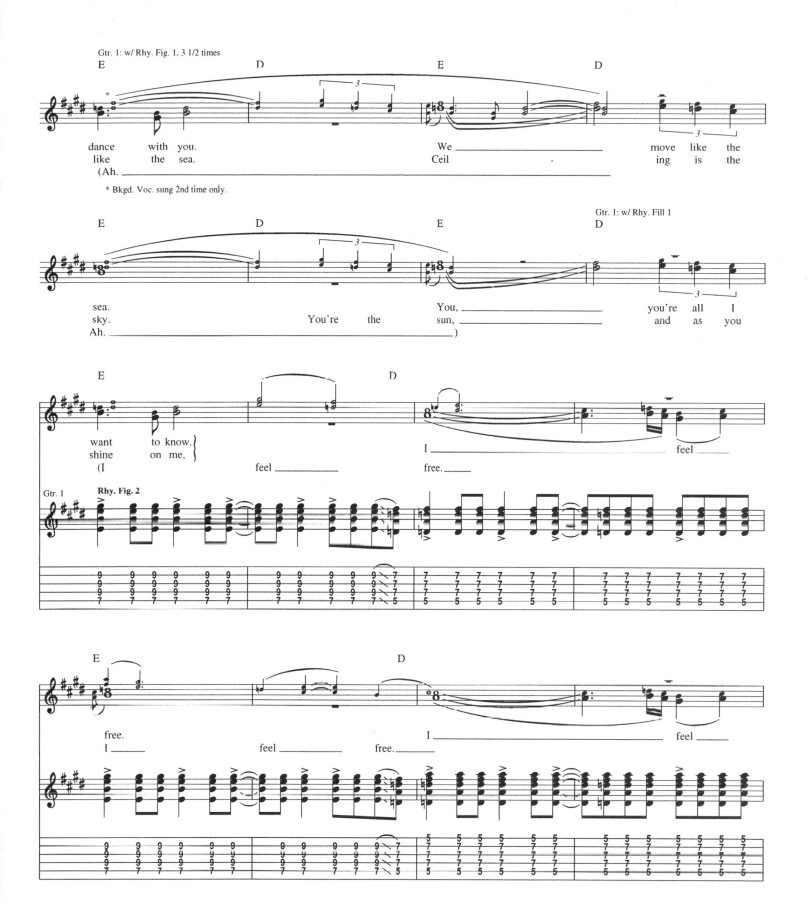

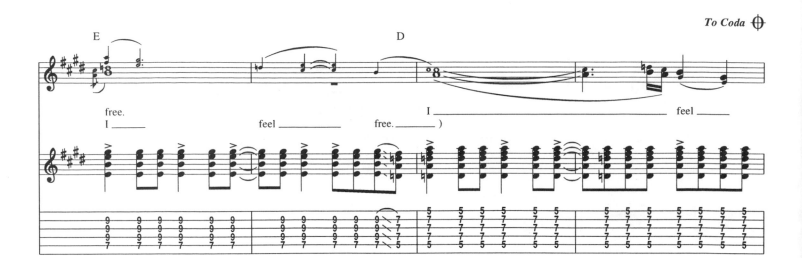

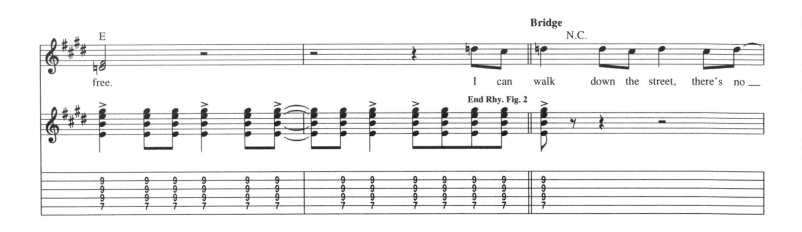

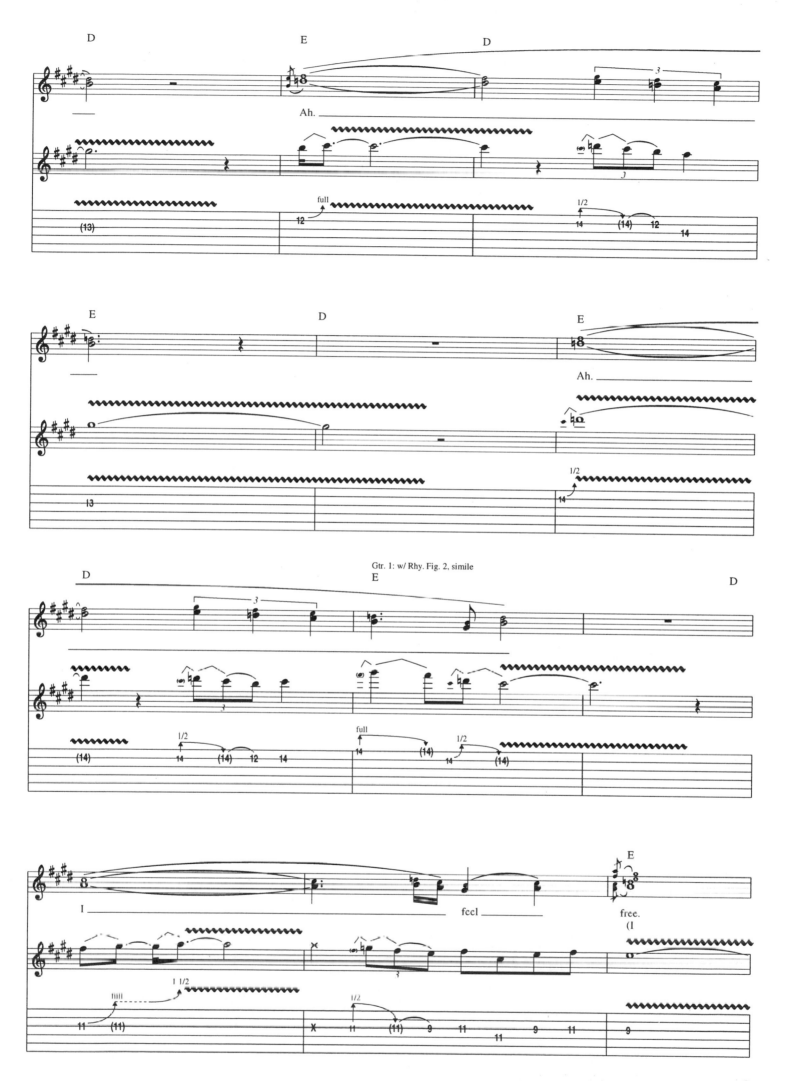

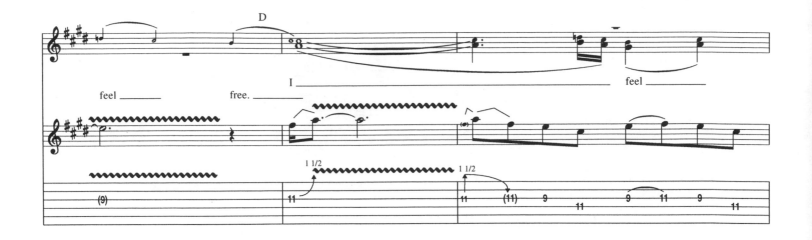

feel _____ free. _____ I _____ feel _____

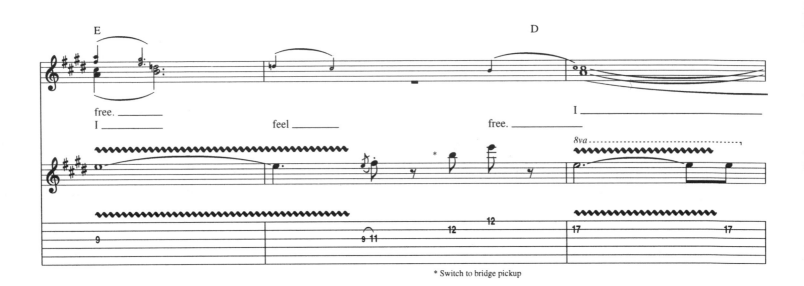

free. _____   feel _____   free. _____   I _____

I _____

* Switch to bridge pickup

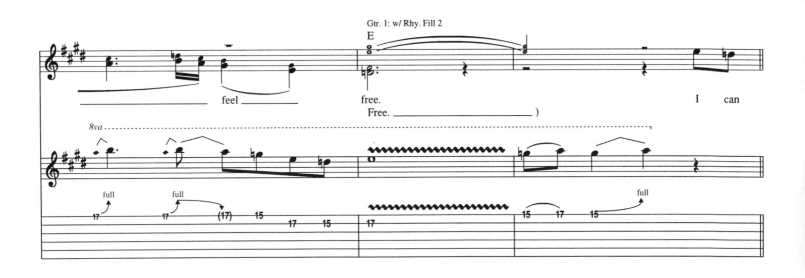

Gtr. 1: w/ Rhy. Fill 2

feel _____   free.   I can

Free. _____)

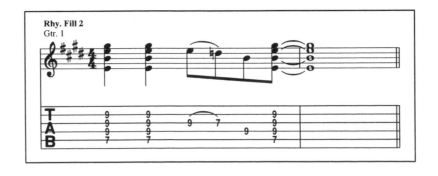

Rhy. Fill 2
Gtr. 1

The Sunshine of Your Love

Words and Music by Jack Bruce, Pete Brown and Eric Clapton

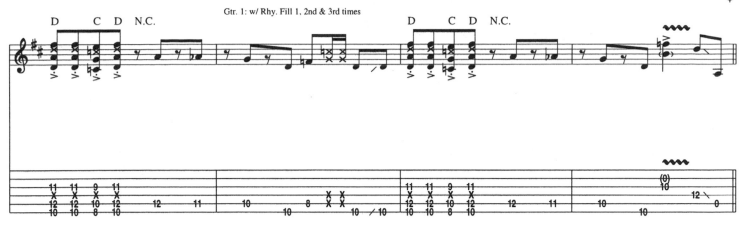

Chorus

I've __ been wait - ing so __ long   to __ be where __ I'm go - ing

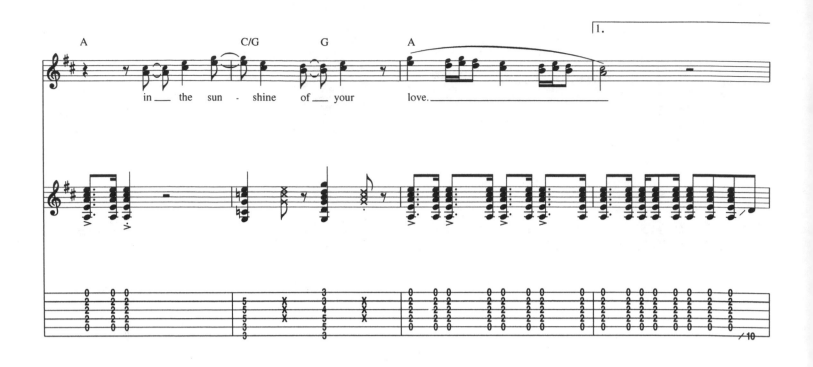

in the sun - shine of your love.

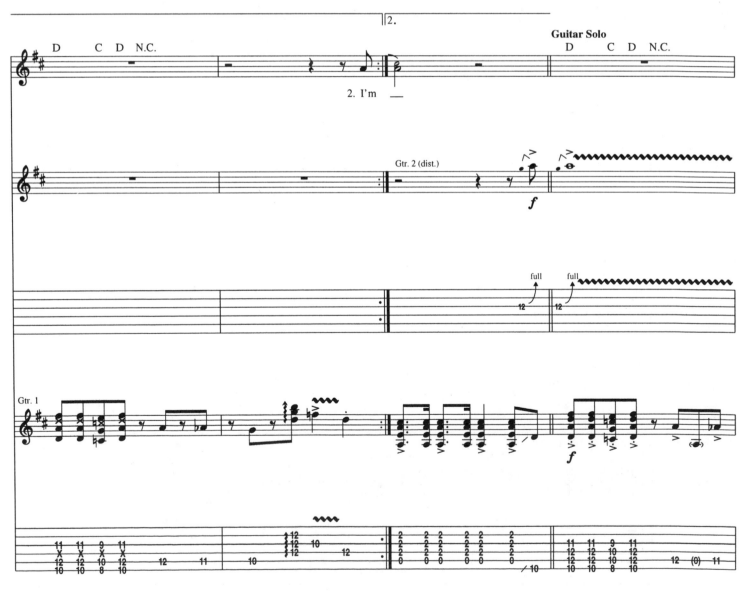

2. I'm

Guitar Solo

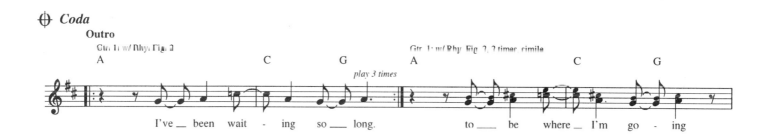

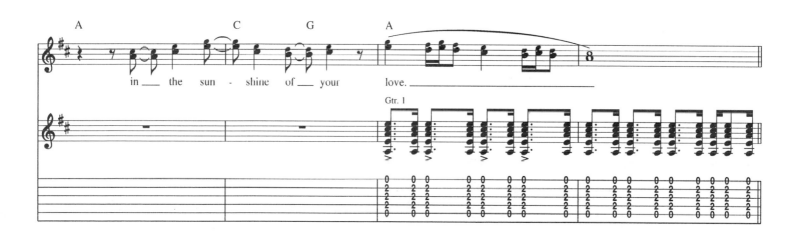

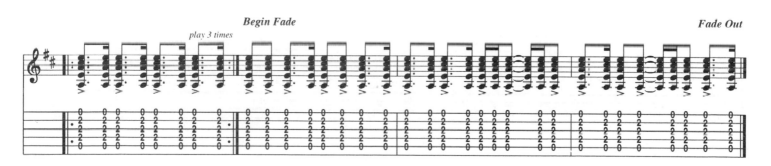

White Room

Words and Music by Jack Bruce and Pete Brown

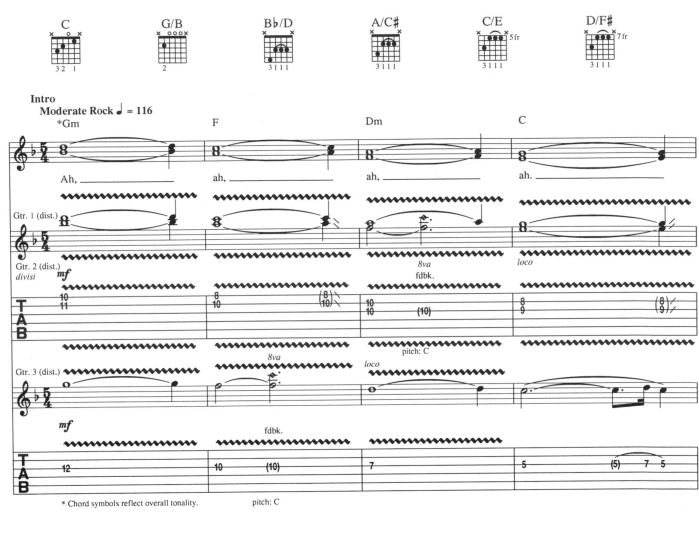

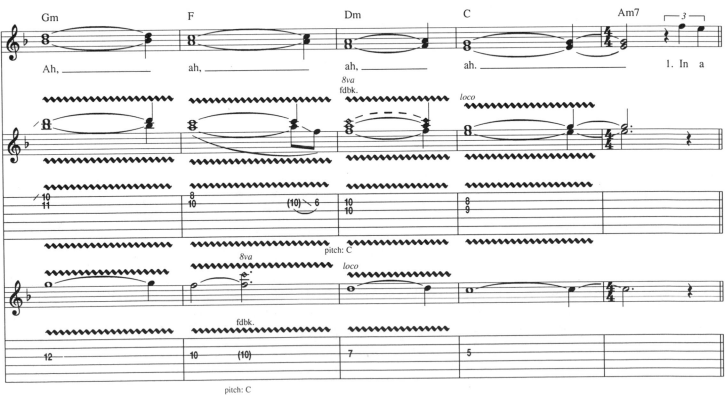

Verse

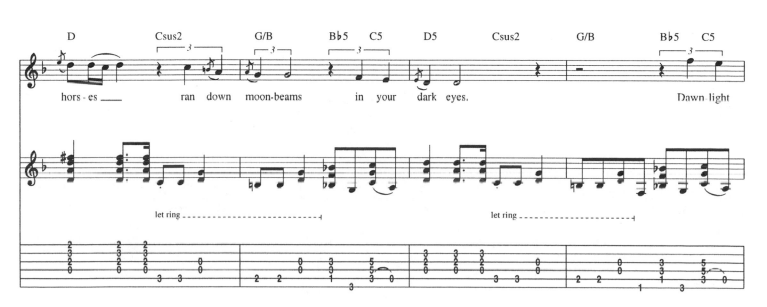

smiles __ on you leav - ing my con - tent - ment. I'll __

Bridge

__ wait __ in this place where the sun _____ nev - er __ shines, wait _____ in this

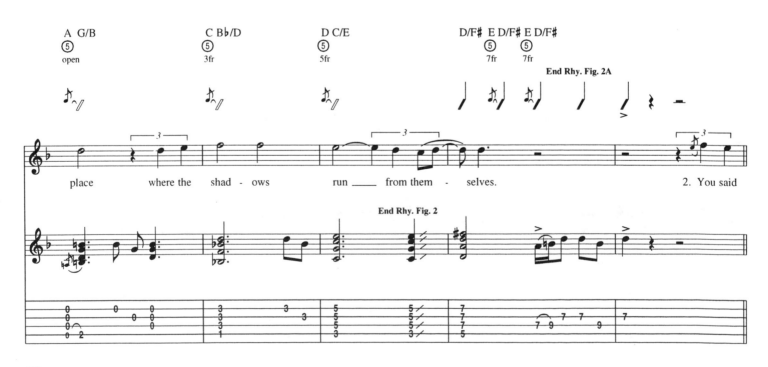

place where the shad - ows run _____ from them - selves. 2. You said

Verse

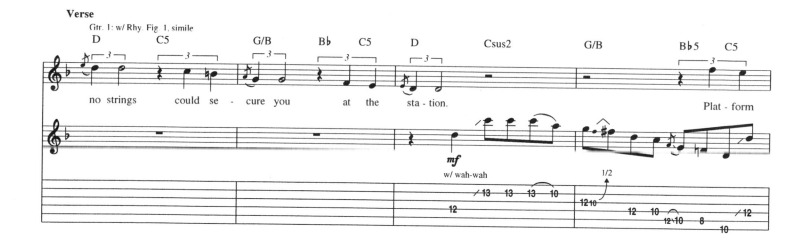

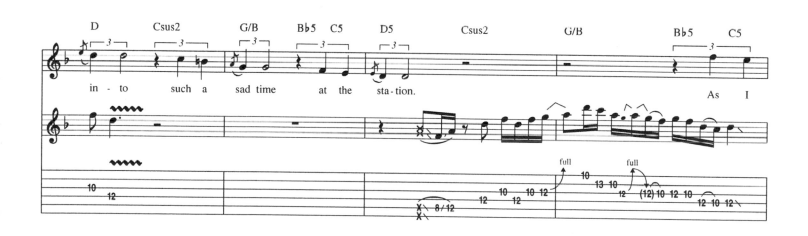

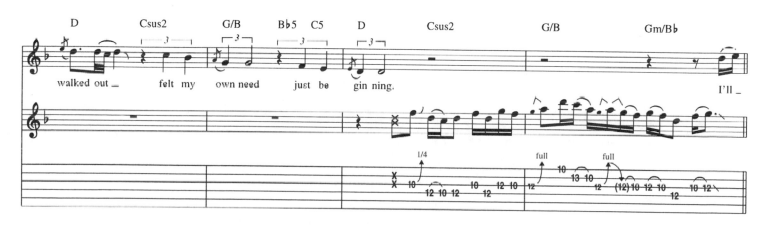

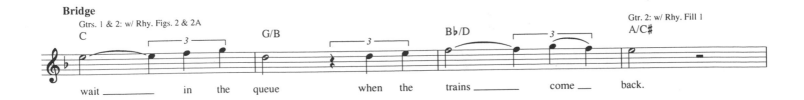

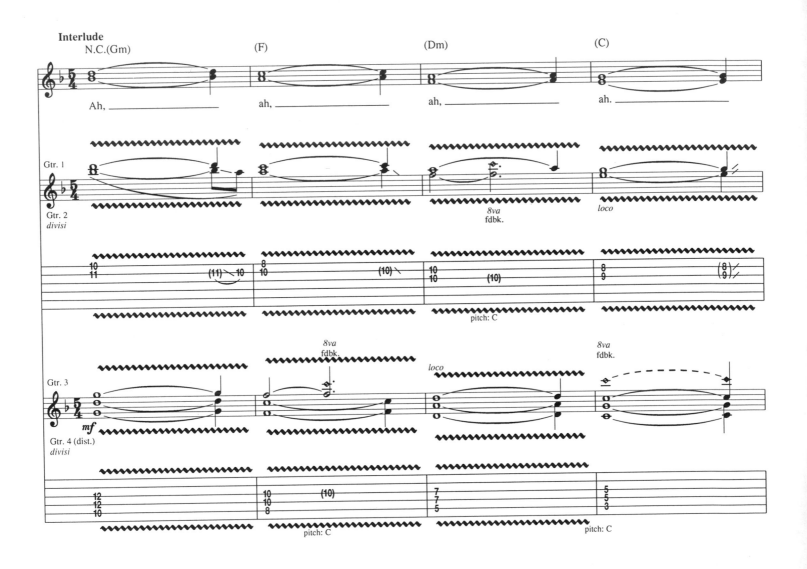

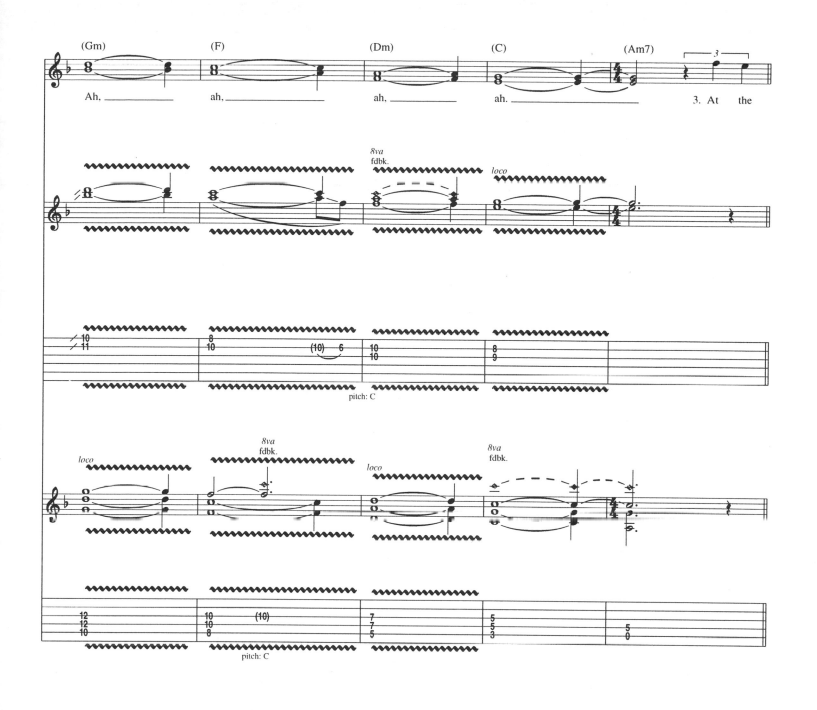

Verse

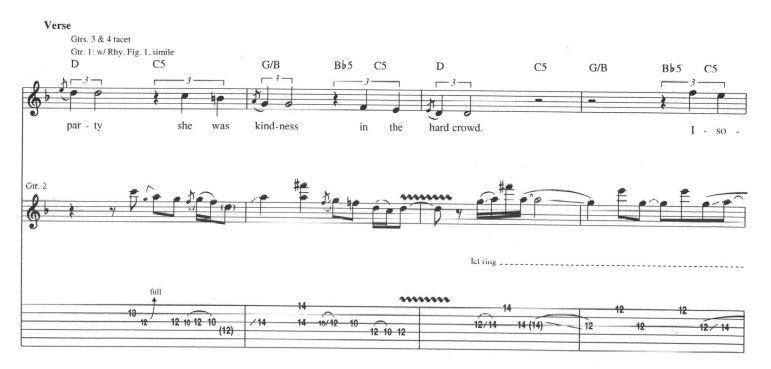

Gtrs. 3 & 4 tacet
Gtr. 1: w/ Rhy. Fig. 1, simile

par - ty she was kind-ness in the hard crowd. I - so -

la - tion   for the   old queen   now for - got - ten.

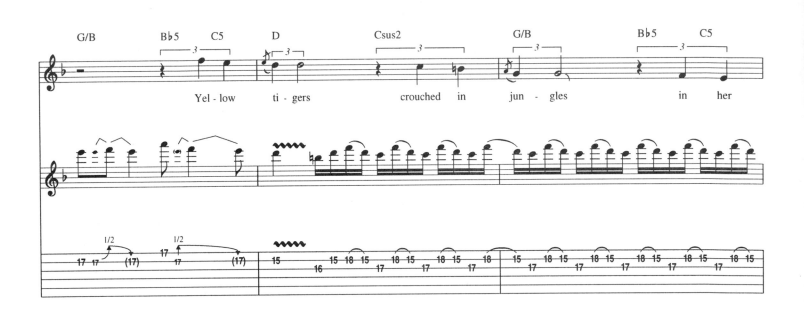

Yel - low   ti - gers   crouched in   jun - gles   in her

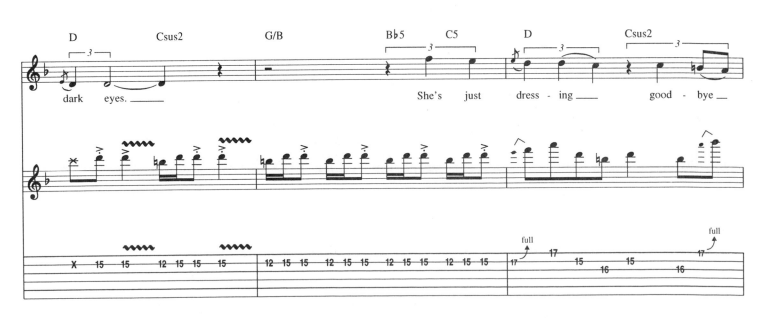

dark   eyes. ____   She's just   dress - ing ____   good - bye ____

win - dows,   tired ___ star - ling. ___   I'll

Bridge

sleep ___ in this place   with the lone - ly ___ crowd.

Lie ___ in the dark,   where the shad - ows run   from them -

Interlude

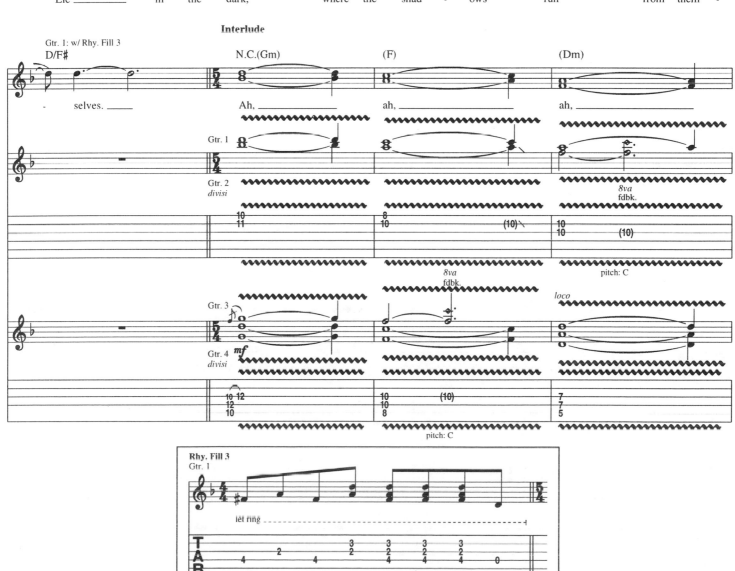

- selves. ___   Ah, ___   ah, ___   ah,

Rhy. Fill 3
Gtr. 1

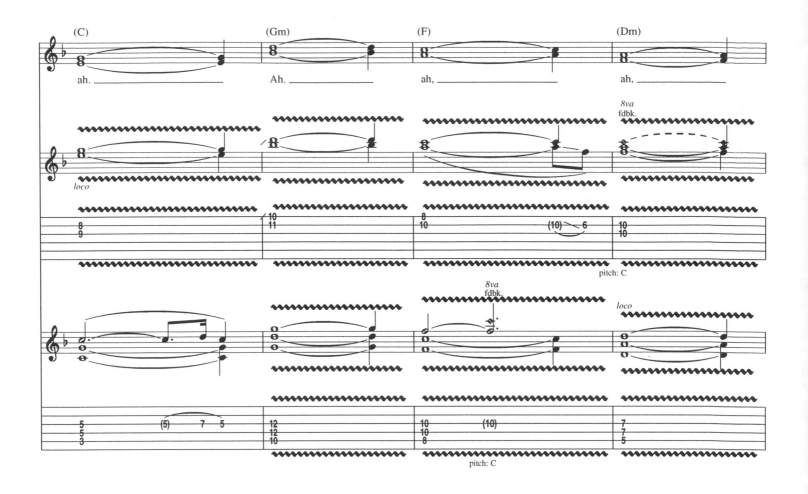

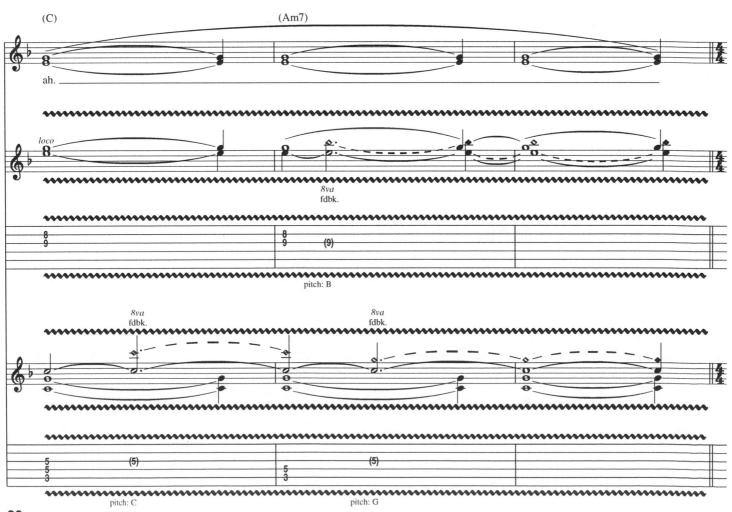

Outro-Guitar Solo

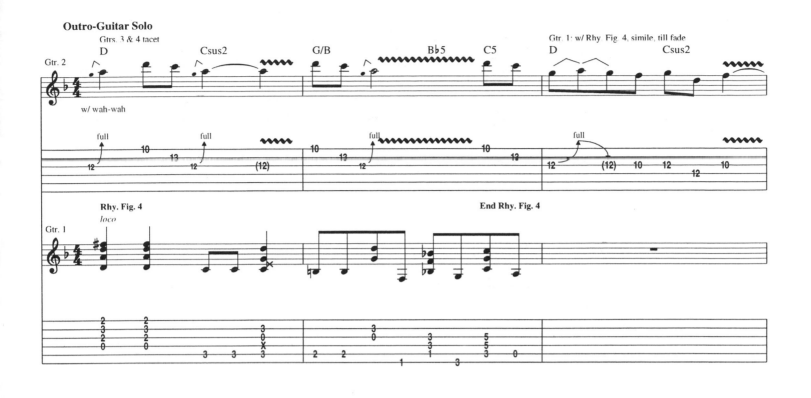

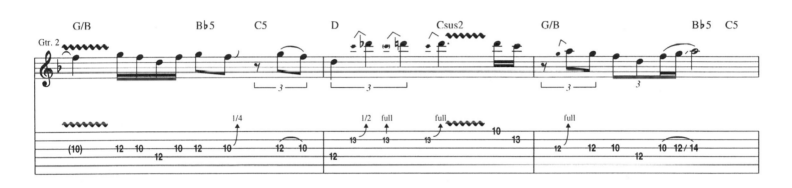

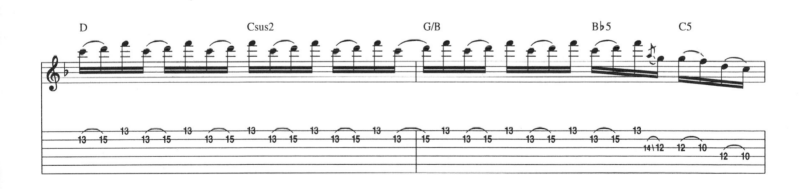

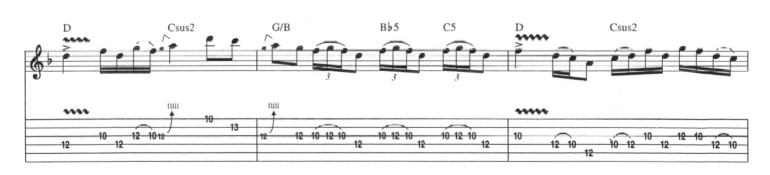

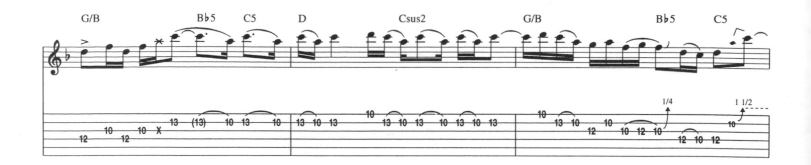

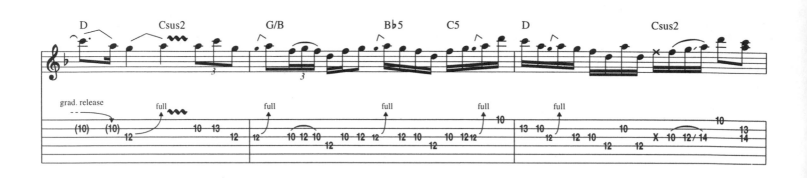

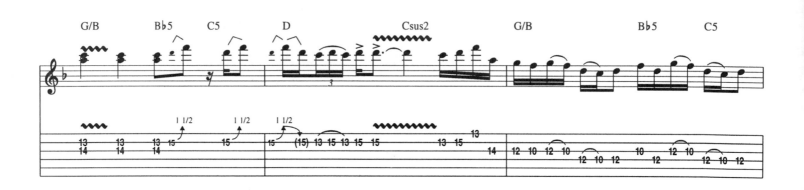

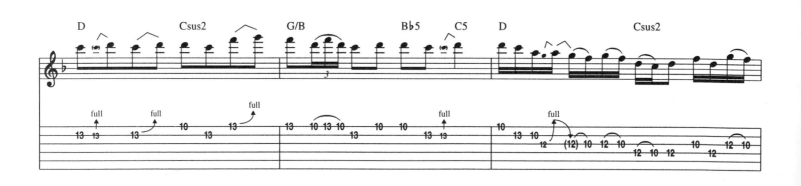

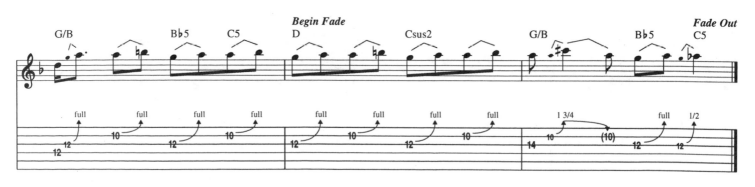

Crossroads
(Cross Road Blues)
Words and Music by Robert Johnson

Intro
Moderately Fast Rock ♩ = 130

Gtr. 1 (dist.) *A

*Chord symbols reflect overall tonality throughout.

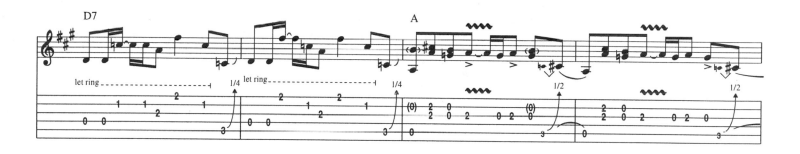

1. I went down

% Verse

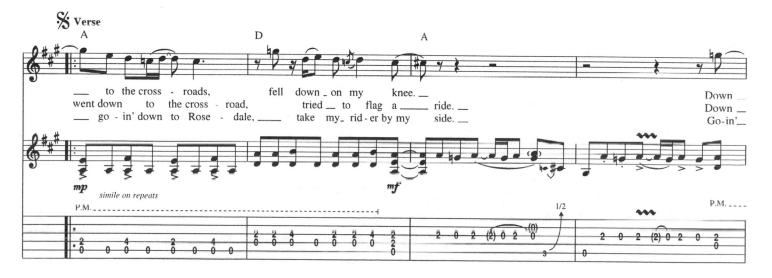

— to the cross - roads, fell down on my knee. — Down —
went down to the cross - road, tried — to flag a — ride. — Down —
— go - in' down to Rose - dale, — take my - rid - er by my side. — Go - in'

Badge

Words and Music by Eric Clapton and George Harrison

they bring the cur - tain down. ____ Yes, be - fore ____ they bring the cur - tain down.

Guitar Solo
Gtr. 2: w/ Rhy. Fig. 2, 3 1/4 times, simile
Gtr. 1: w/ Rhy. Fig. 3, 3 1/4 times, simile

Woo. ____

Yea,   yea,   yea. ____

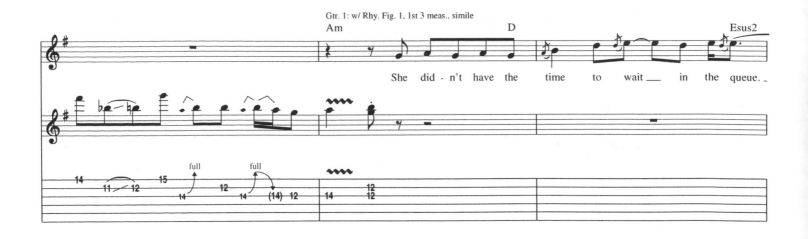

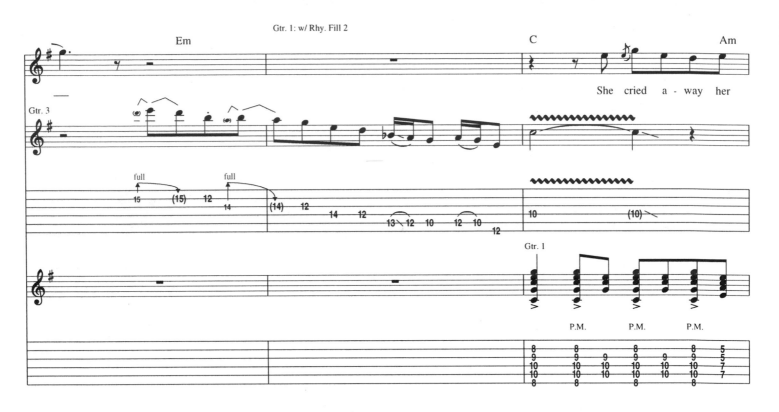

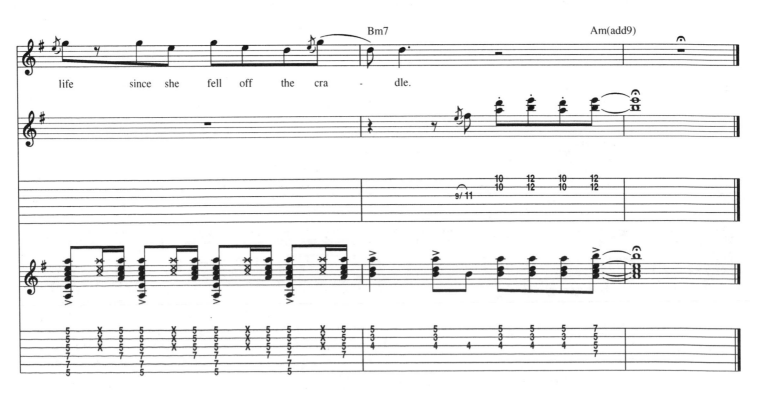

38

Presence of the Lord

Words and Music by Eric Clapton

just like I nev-er could be - fore. _____

And I ___ know I don't _ have   much _____ to   give, _____

but soon   I'll o - pen an - y   door. _____

Ev - 'ry - bod - y knows the se - cret. _____

Guitar Solo
Double-Time ♩ = 135

Gtr. 1: w/ Rhy. Fig. 1, 5 times, simile

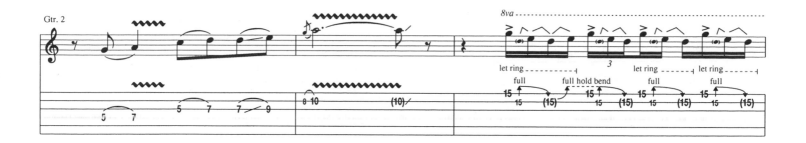

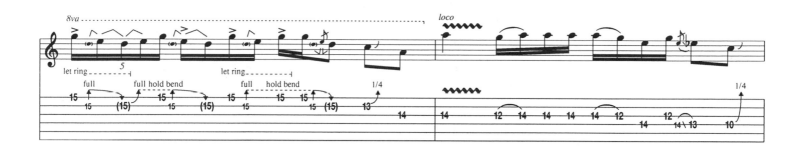

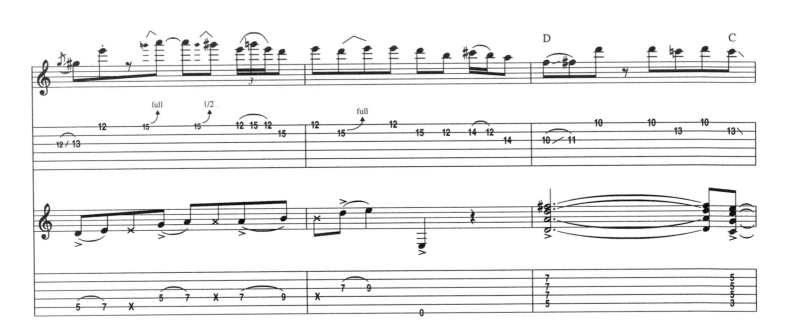

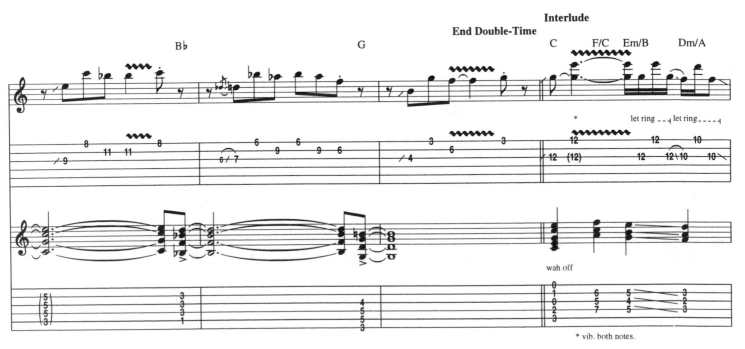

45

Blues Power

Words and Music by Eric Clapton and Leon Russell

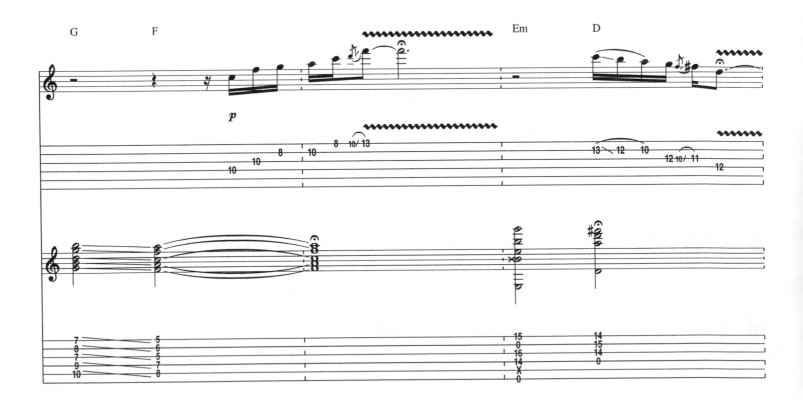

Verse
Moderate Rock ♩ = 150

1.Bet you did-n't think I knew how to rock and roll.

Gtr. 1

Gtr. 2

Rhy. Fig. 1

P.M.

Lord, I've got the boog-ie woog-ie right down in my

let ring   let ring

P.M.   P.M.

P.M.   P.M.

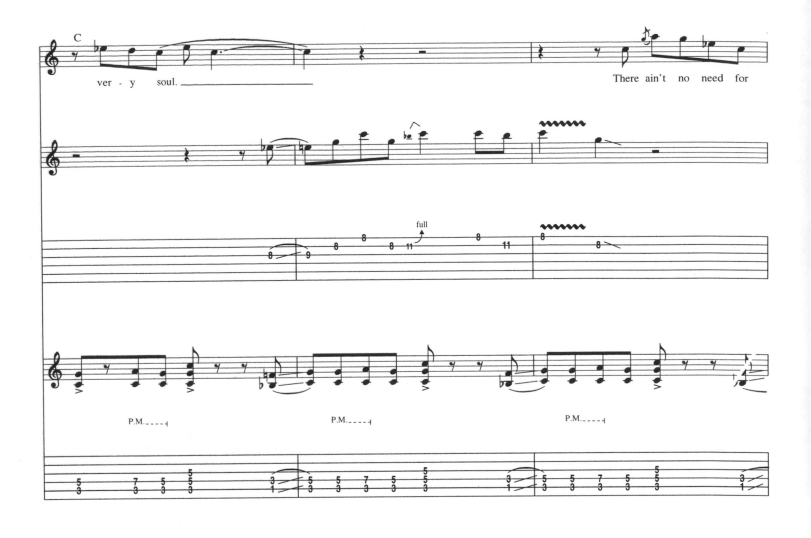

ver - y soul. _____ There ain't no need for

me   to   be   a   wall - flow   - er, _____

'cause now I'm ___ liv - in' on blues ___ pow - er.

Guitar Solo

End Rhy. Fig. 1

Rhy. Fig. 2

End Rhy. Fig. 2

* Gtr. 1 doubled next 6 meas.

'cause now I'm ___ liv - in' on blues ___ pow, pow - er.

Guitar Solo

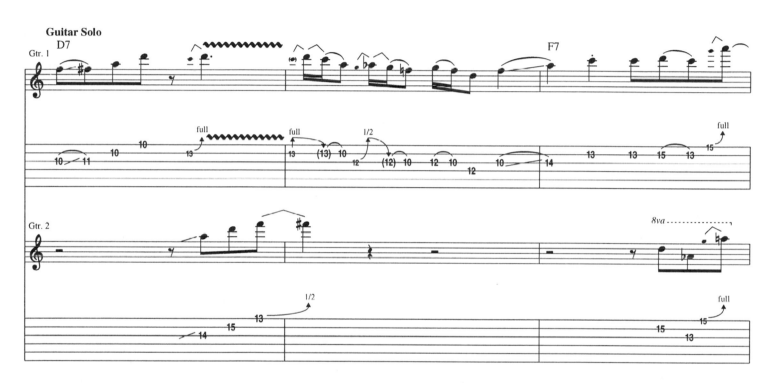

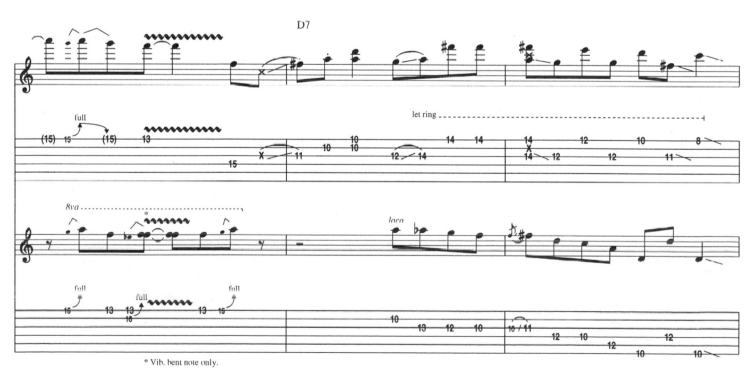

* Vib. bent note only.

Outro

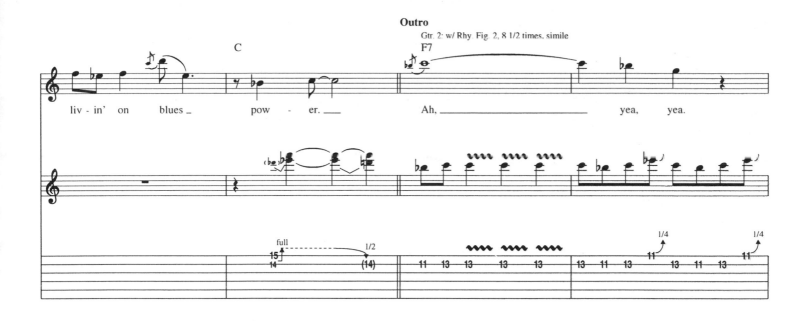

liv- in' on blues _ pow - er. ___ Ah, _____ yea, yea.

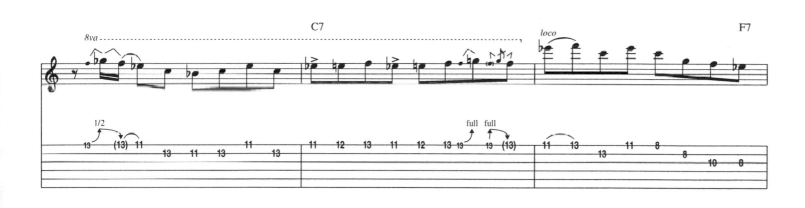

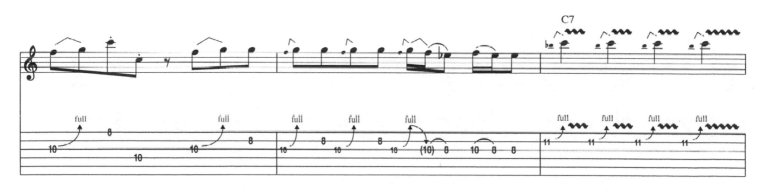

After Midnight

Words and Music by John J. Cale

Guitar Solo

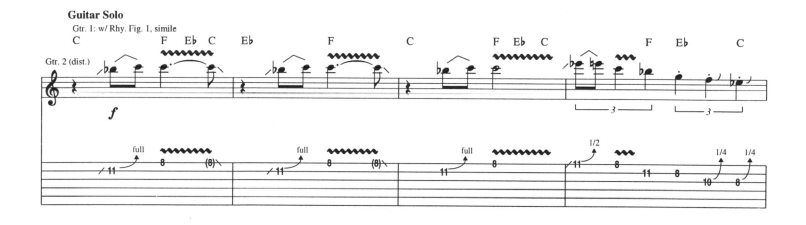

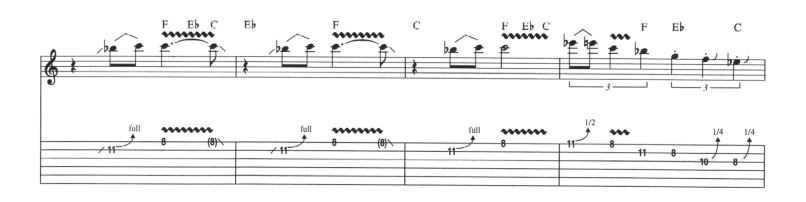

(Gon - na let it all _ hang down._)

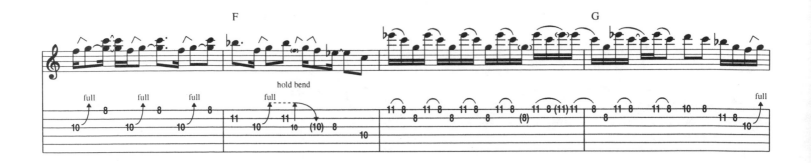

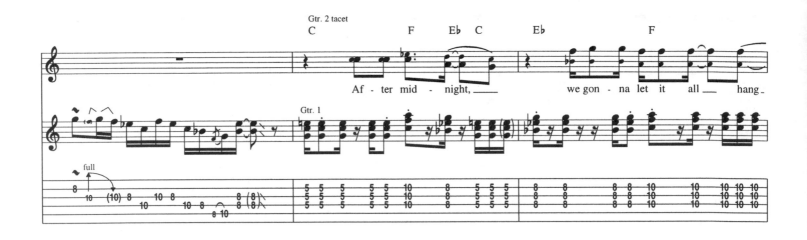

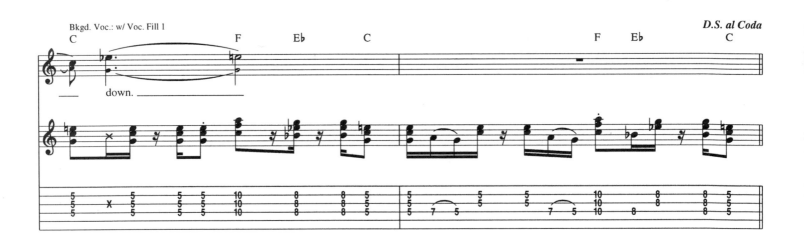

Coda

Let It Rain

Words and Music by Eric Clapton and Bonnie Bramlett

Gtr. 4: w/ Rhy. Fig. 1

1. The

𝄋 Verse

Gtrs. 1 & 2 tacet

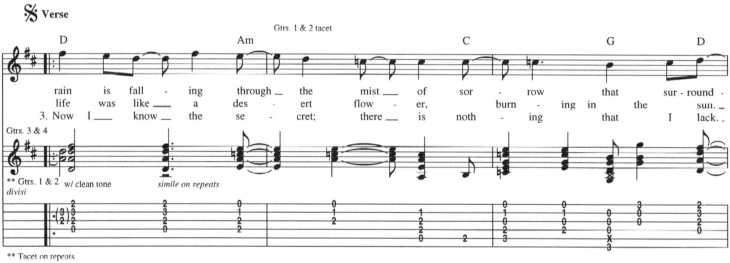

rain is fall — ing through ___ the mist ___ of sor — row that sur — round —
life was like ___ a des — ert flow — er, burn — ing in the sun. ___
3. Now I ___ know ___ the se — cret; there ___ is noth — ing that I lack. ___

Gtrs. 3 & 4

** Gtrs. 1 & 2 w/ clean tone
divisi
simile on repeats

** Tacet on repeats

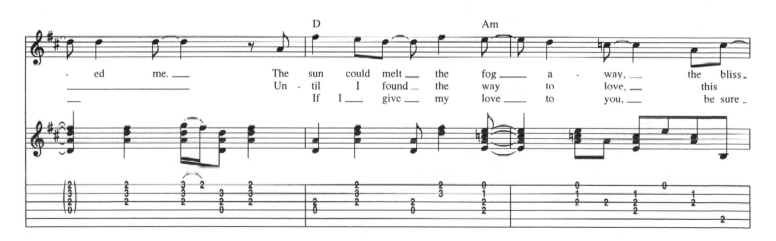

— ed me. ___ The sun could melt ___ the fog ___ a — way, ___ the bliss. ___
Un — til I found ___ the way to love, ___ this
___ If I ___ give ___ my love ___ to you, ___ be sure ___

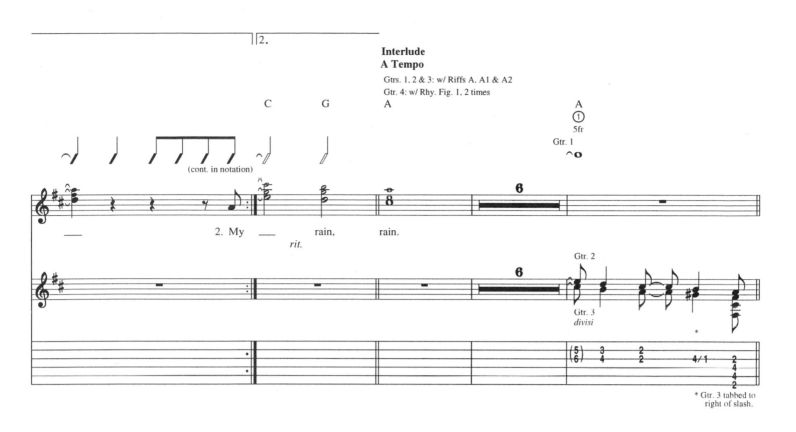

Interlude
A Tempo

Gtrs. 1, 2 & 3: w/ Riffs A, A1 & A2
Gtr. 4: w/ Rhy. Fig. 1, 2 times

2. My ___ rain, rain.

rit.

* Gtr. 3 tabbed to right of slash.

Guitar Solo

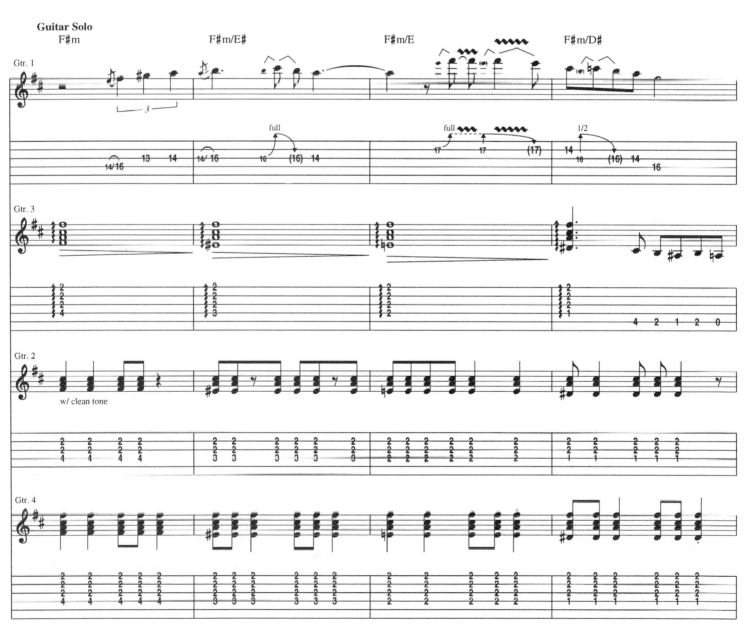

66

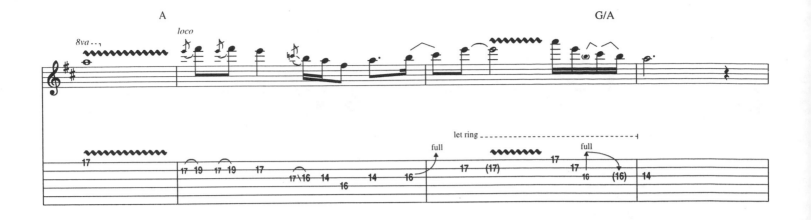

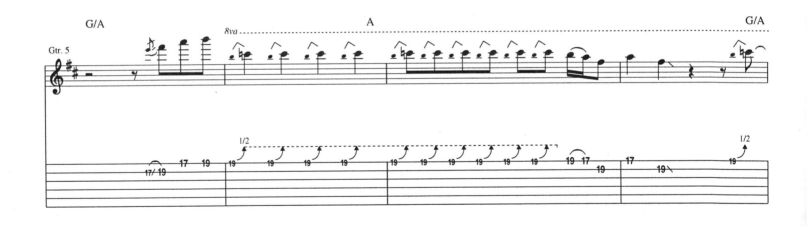

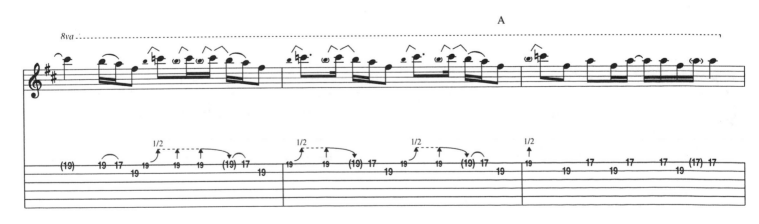

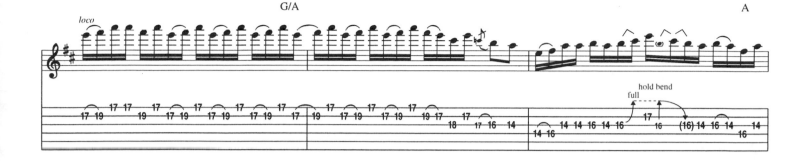

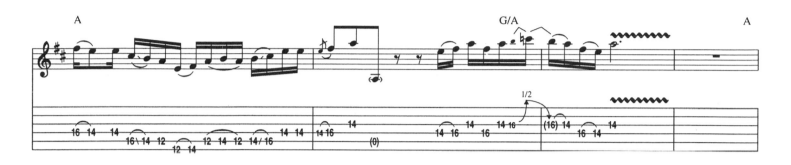

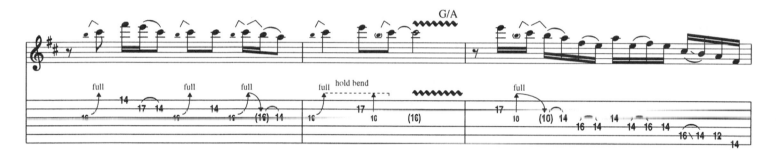

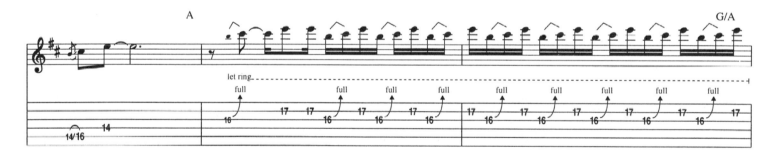

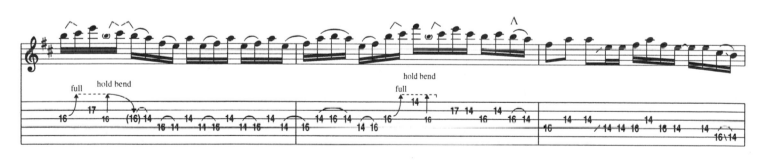

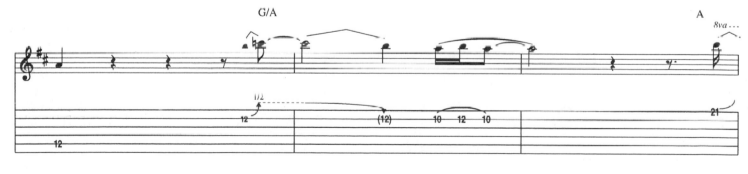

Bell Bottom Blues

Words and Music by Eric Clapton

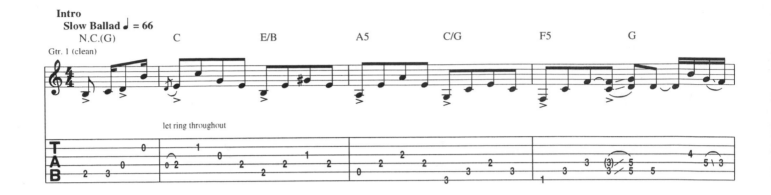

74

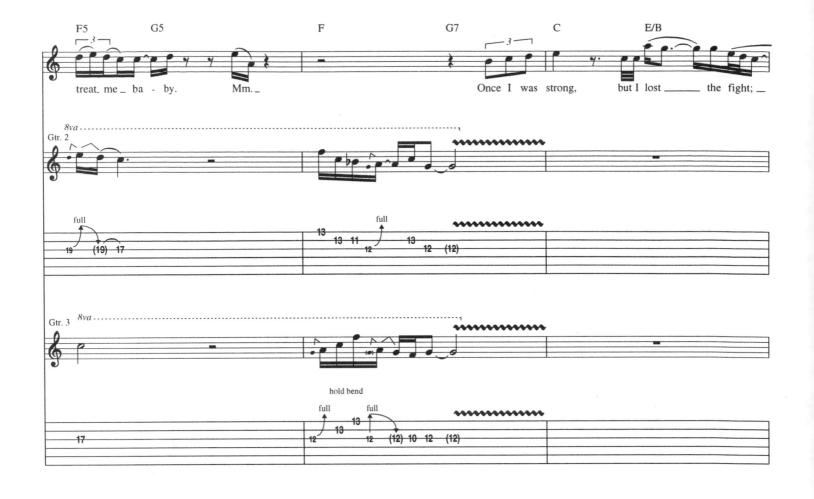

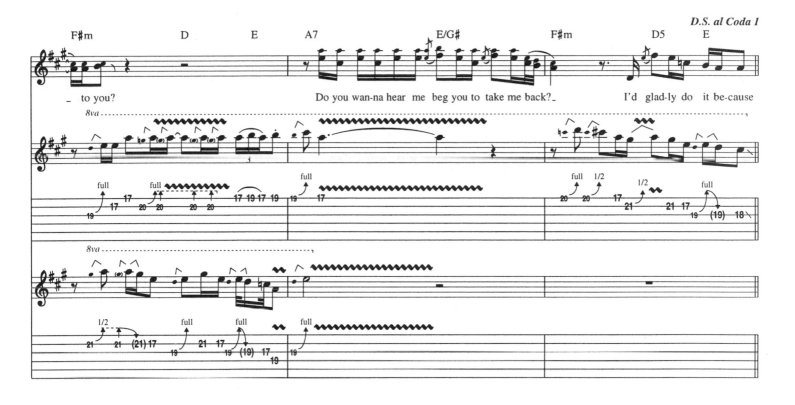

to you?   Do you wan-na hear me beg you to take me back?   I'd glad-ly do it be-cause

Coda 1

Guitar Solo

Gtrs. 2 & 3 tacet
Gtr. 1: w/ Rhy. Fig. 1, simile

Gtrs. 1, 2 & 3: w/ Rhy. Fills 1, 1A & 1B

D - d - d - do

Gtr. 4 (dist.)

Gtr. 2: w/ Fill 1

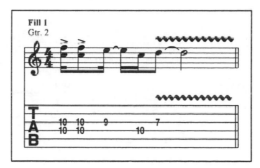

Fill 1
Gtr. 2

Do you wan-na see me crawl a - cross the floor

D.S. al Coda 2

— to you?   Do you wan-na hear me beg you to take me back?__   I'd glad - ly do__ it 'cause

✛ _Coda 2_

Verse

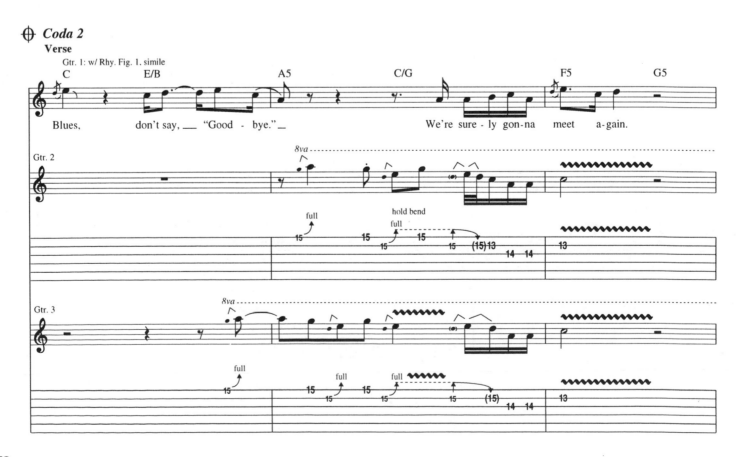

Blues,   don't say, __ "Good - bye." __   We're sure - ly gon-na meet a-gain.

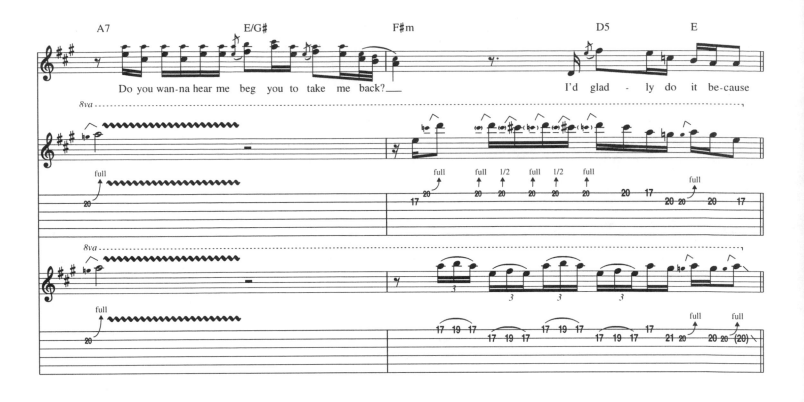

Do you wan-na hear me beg you to take me back?___ I'd glad - ly do it be-cause

Outro-Chorus

Gtr. 1: w/ Rhy. Fig. 3, simile
Gtrs. 2 & 3: w/ Riffs A & A1

I don't wan-na fade a - way.___ Give me one more day, ___ please. ___ I don't want to fade a - way.___

In your heart ___ I want ___ to stay.

Layla

Words and Music by Eric Clapton and Jim Gordon

* Composite arr. Gtr. 6 mixed down on this recording. It is easier to hear on previous releases.

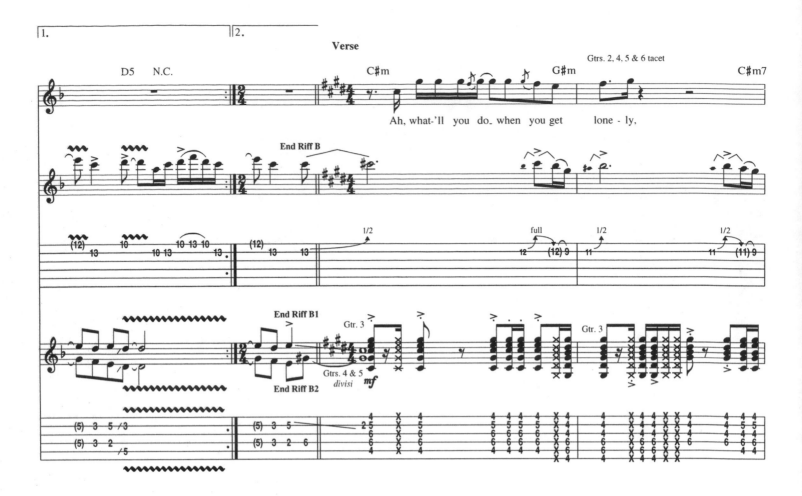

Ah, what-'ll you do when you get lone - ly,

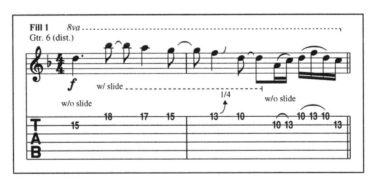

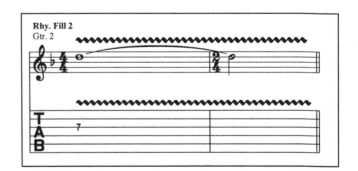

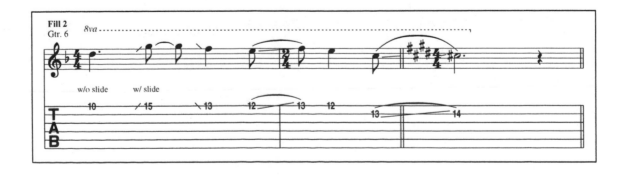

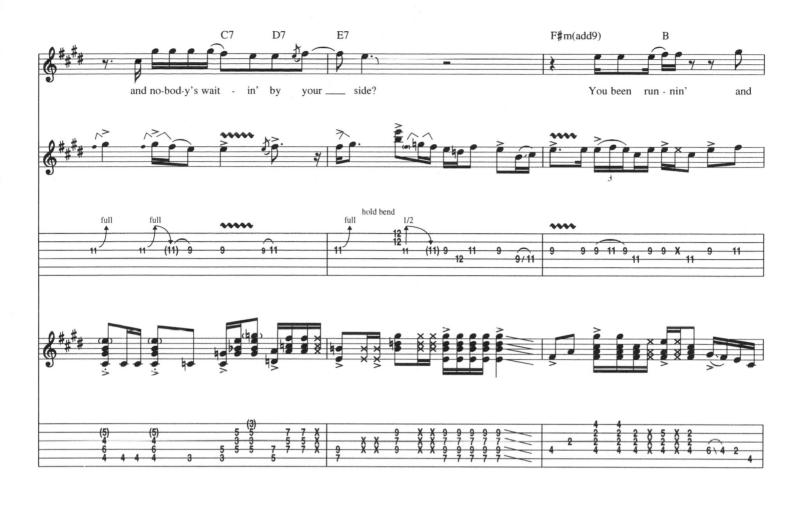

and no-bod-y's wait - in' by your ___ side? You been run - nin' and

hid - in' much_too long, ___ you know it's just_your fool - ish pride.

(Lay -

𝄋 Chorus

Gtrs. 1, 4 & 5: w/ Riffs B, B1 & B2, 1st & 2nd times;
    w/ Riffs B, B1 & B2, 1st 7 meas, 3rd time
Gtr. 2: w/ Riff A, 3 times
Gtr. 3: w/ Rhy. Fig. 1, 3 times
Gtr. 6: w/ Fill 3, 1st time; w/ Riff B, 1st 4 meas, 2nd time;
    w/ Riff B, 1st 2 meas., 3rd time

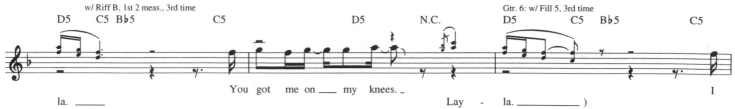

You got me on ___ my knees. ___   Lay - la. _____)   I

la. _____

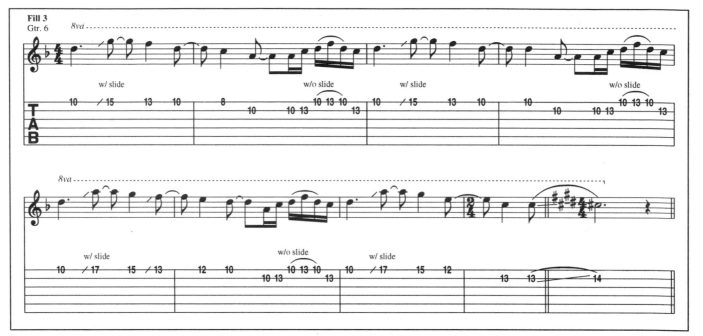

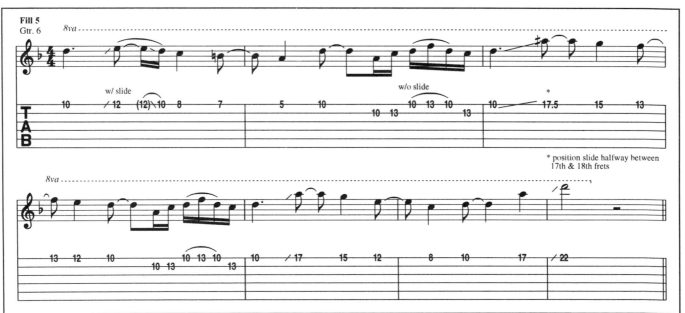

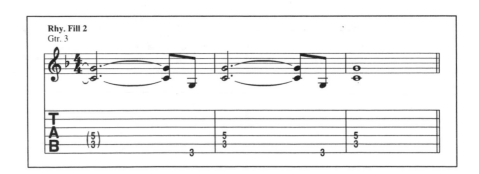

you turned my whole world up - side down.

(Lay

Coda 1
Verse

3. So make the best of the sit - u - a - tion, be-fore I fin' n'ly go in -

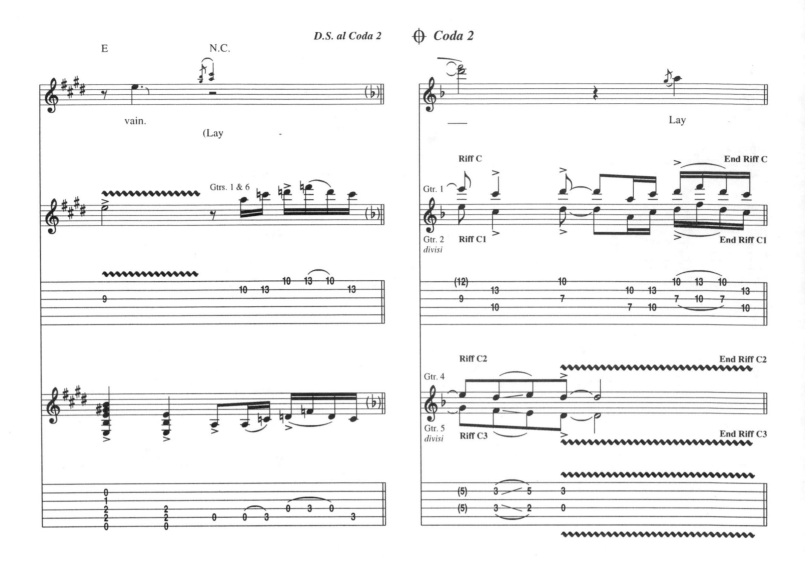

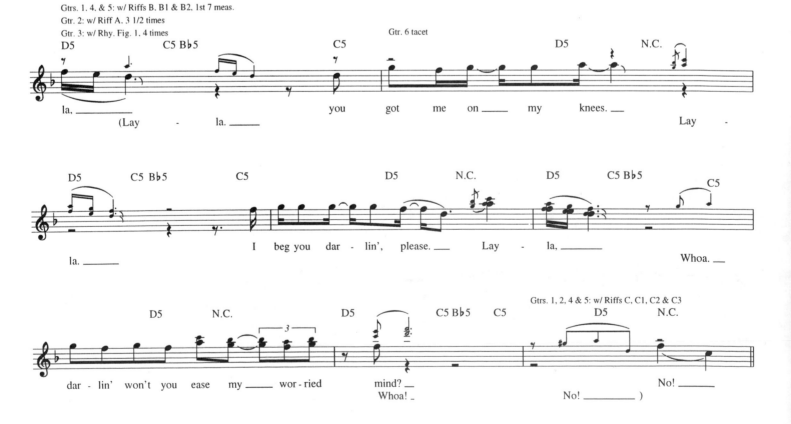

Guitar Solo

Gtrs. 1, 4, & 5: w/ Riffs B, B1 & B2, 1st 7 meas.
Gtr. 2: w/ Riff A, 3 1/2 times
Gtr. 3: w/ Rhy. Fig. 1, 11 1/2 times, simile

* TAB numbers based on location of notes beyond fretboard.

Gtrs. 1, 2, 4 & 5: w/ Riffs C, C1, C2 & C3

Gtrs. 1, 4 & 5: w/ Riffs B, B1 & B2, 1st 7 meas.
Gtr. 2: w/ Riff A, 3 1/2 times

Gtrs. 1, 2, 4 & 5: w/ Riffs C, C1, C2, & C3

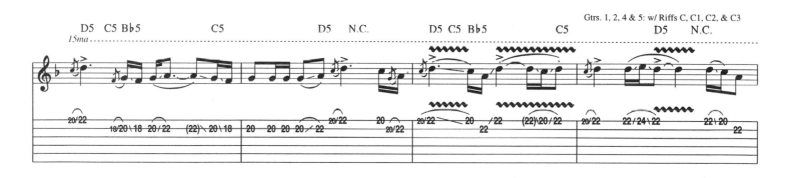

Gtrs. 1, 4 & 5: w/ Riffs B, B1 & B2, 1st 7 meas.
Gtr. 2: w/ Riff A, 3 1/2 times

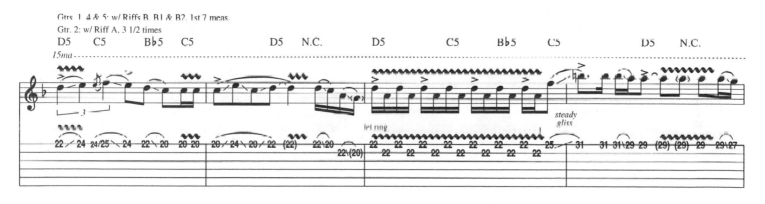

*Chord symbols come from piano.

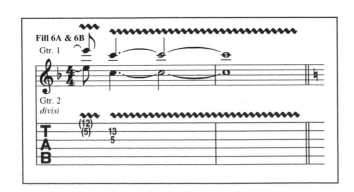

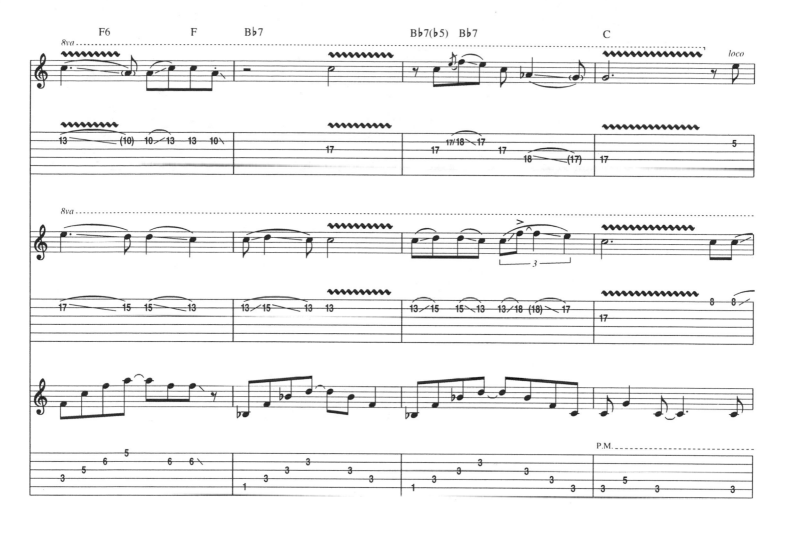

Gtr. 7: w/ Rhy. Fig. 2, 1st 5 meas., simile

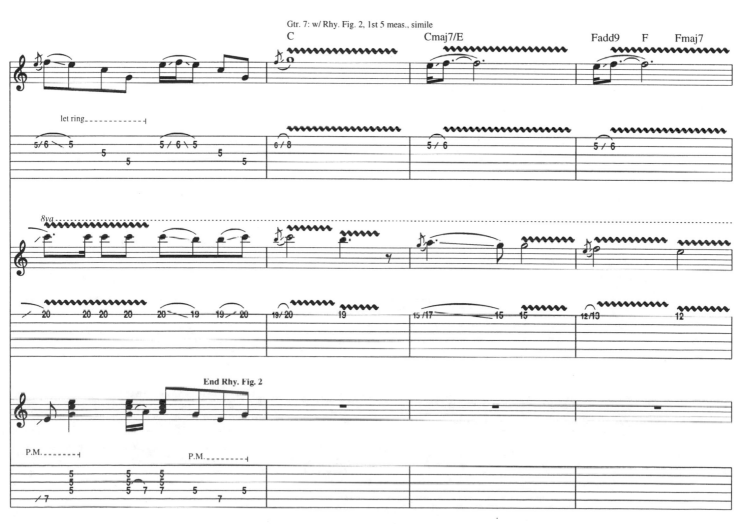

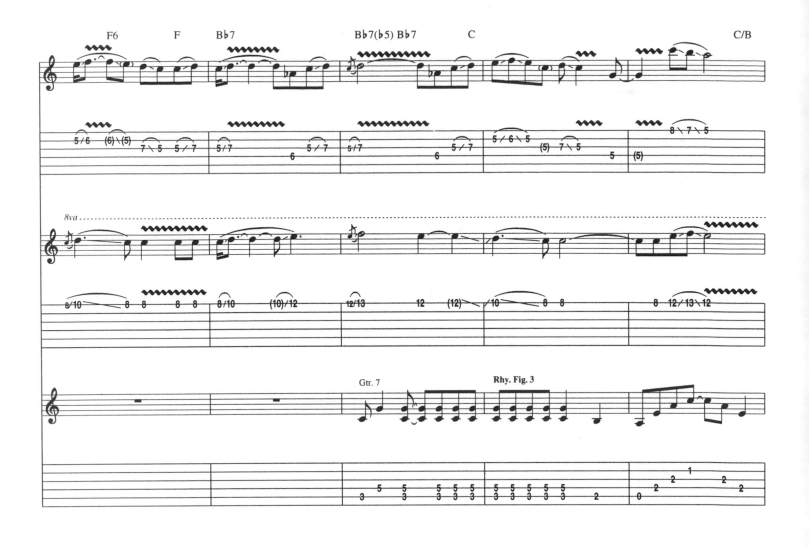

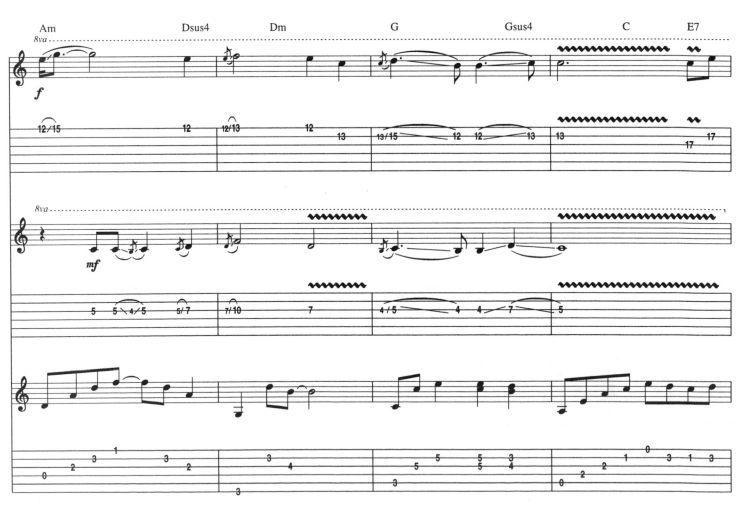

94

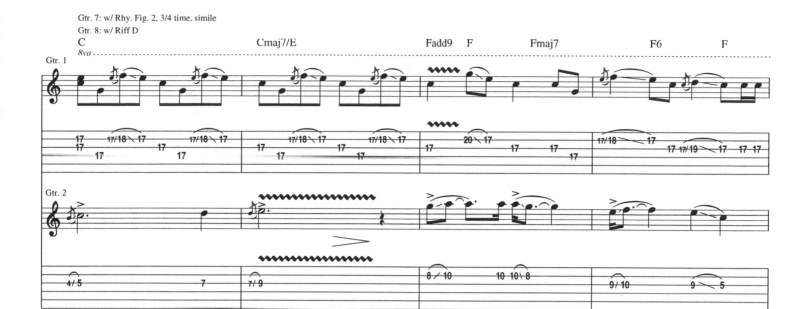

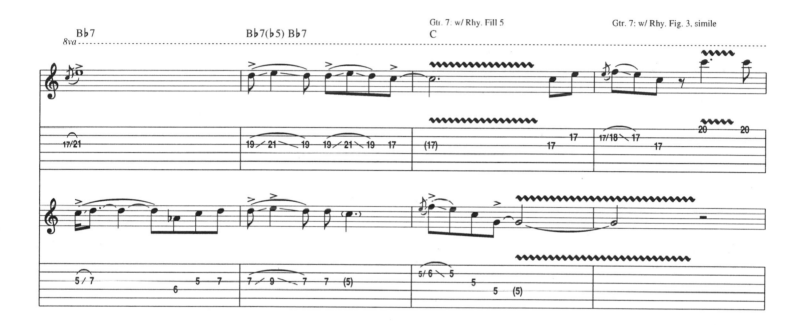

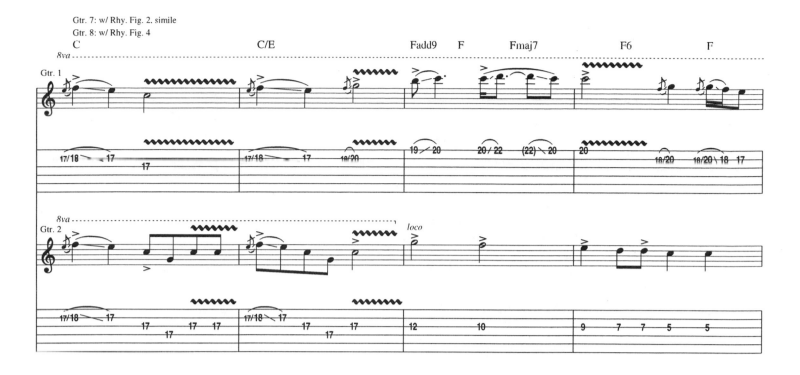

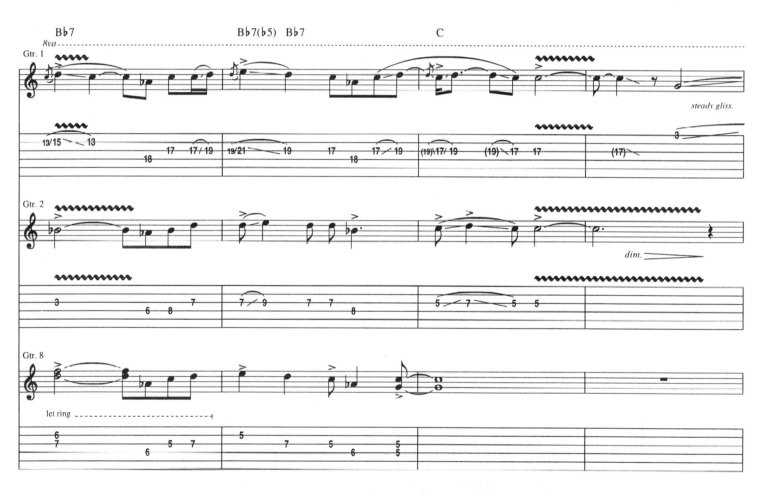

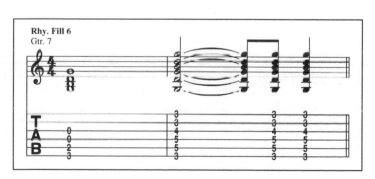

98

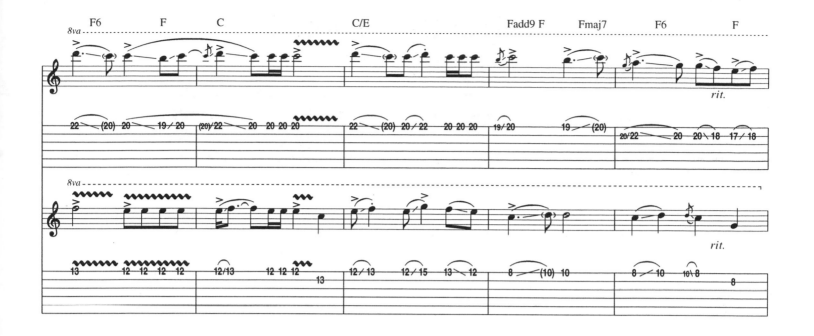

I Shot the Sheriff

Words and Music by Bob Marley

* sung behind the beat.

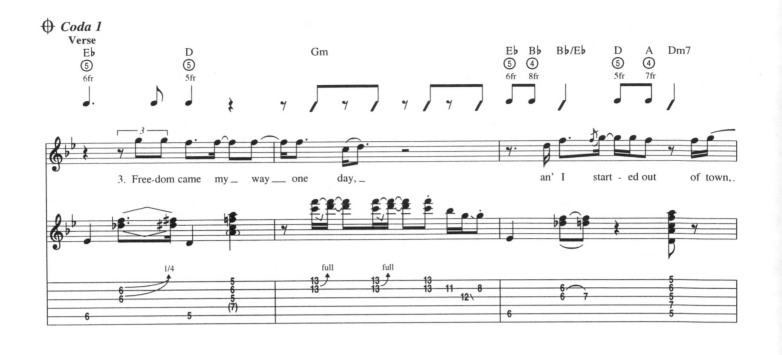

108

Let It Grow

Words and Music by Eric Clapton

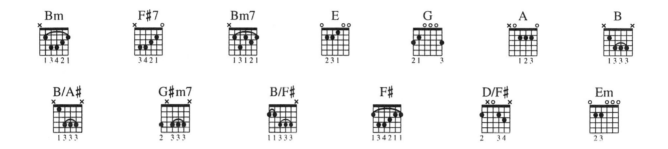

Gtr. 4; Open G Tuning:
① = D ④ = D
② = D ⑤ = G
③ = G ⑥ = D

Verse
Moderately ♩ = 78

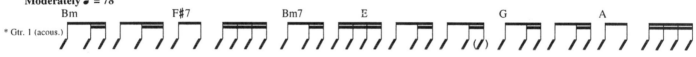

* Gtr. 1 (acous.)

1. Stand-ing at __ the cross - roads, try'n' to read __ the signs to tell me which way I should

* Two acous. (6-str. & 12-str. gtrs.) arr. for one.

go to find __ the an - swer, __ and all the time __ I __ know, plant your love and let __ it

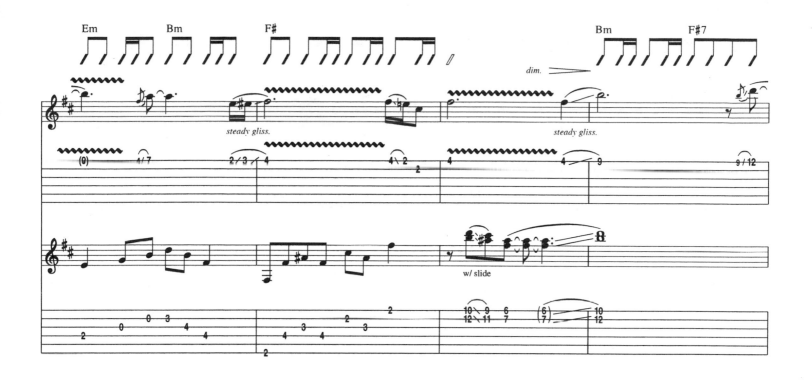

3. Time is get-ting short - er. There's

* Composite arr.

much for you __ to __ do. On - ly ask, __ and you. will __ get what you are need - ing. The

rest is up to __ you. Plant your love __ and let __ it __ grow.

Chorus

simile on repeat

Let it grow, let it grow. _____ Let it blos-som, let __ it

simile on repeat

114

Knockin' on Heaven's Door

Words and Music by Bob Dylan

* Harmony tacet on 2nd Verse

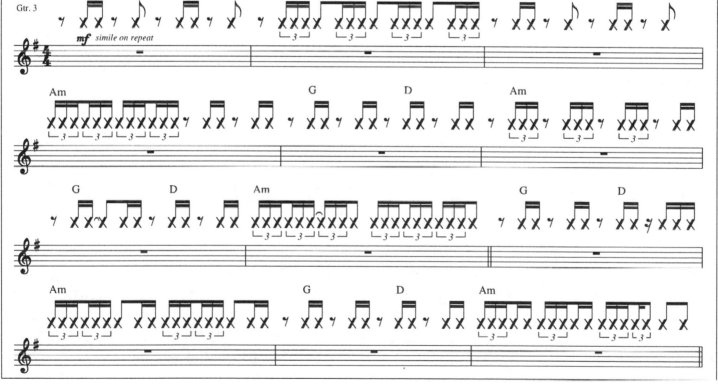

It's get - tin' dark __ too dark to see.
There's a long black cloud __ fol - low - in' me.

Feel like I'm knock - in' on heav - en's door. __

Knock, knock, knock - in' on heav - en's door. __

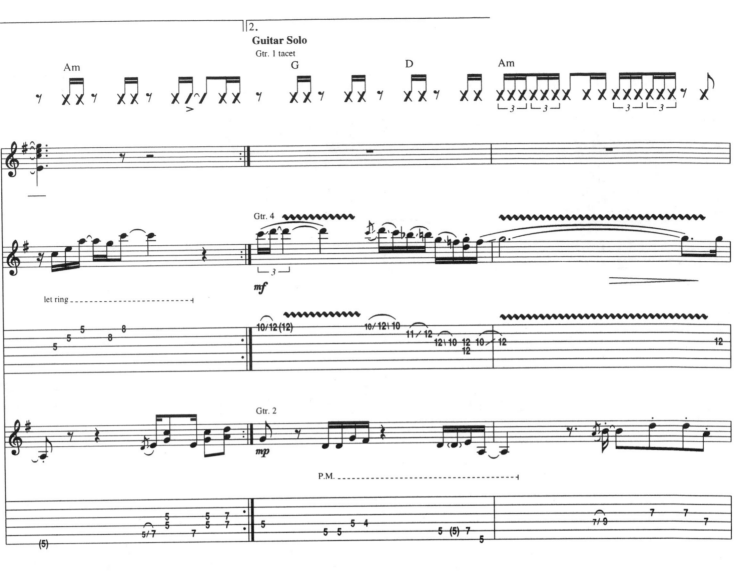

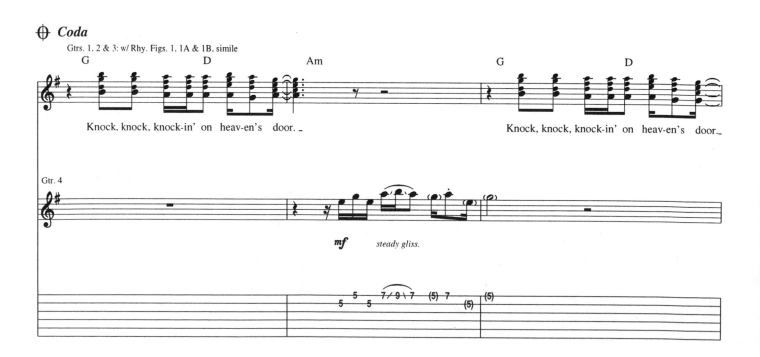

122

Outro

Hello Old Friend

Words and Music by Eric Clapton

Verse

Gtr. 1: w/ Rhy. Fig. 2, 2 3/4 times, simile
Gtr. 2: w/ Riff C, 2 3/4 times, simile
Gtrs. 3 & 4: w/ Fill 2, 2nd time
Gtrs. 3 & 4: w/ Fill 6, 3rd time
G D C Em G
saw a flow - er glow - ing in the dark. It
could - n't stop 'cause I was in a car. I'm
thought I knew him, but I could - n't say. I
Gtr. 3
Gtr. 4

Fill 2
Gtr. 3
full
full
Gtr. 4

Fill 6
Gtr. 3
full
full
Gtr. 4
full
full
full

§ **Chorus**

it's real - ly good_ to see_____ you once a - gain.

(Hel - lo _____ old friend.)

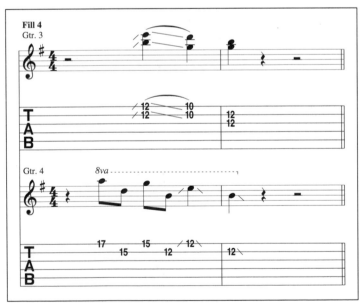

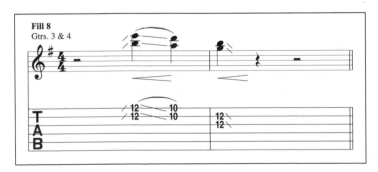

Gtr. 3: w/ Fill 10, 4th time

Gtr. 3: w/ Fill 9, 3rd time
Gtr. 4: w/ Fill 9, 4th time

Em   Bm   Am   C

Hel-lo old friend, _ it's real - ly good _ to see _____ you _ once a - gain.

(Hel - lo _____ old friend,

Gtr. 2

Gtr. 3

Gtr. 1: w/ Rhy. Fig. 1, 2 times, simile
Gtr. 2: w/ Riff A, 2 times, simile
Gtrs. 3 & 4: w/ Riffs B & B1, 1st time, simile
Gtrs. 3 & 4: w/ Riffs B & B1, 1st 7 meas., 2nd & 3rd times, simile

G   D   C   Em   D

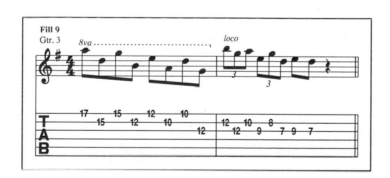

Ah. _____)

Fill 9
Gtr. 3

Fill 10
Gtr. 3

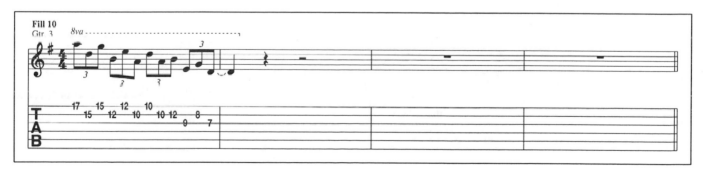

130

Cocaine

Words and Music by John J. Cale

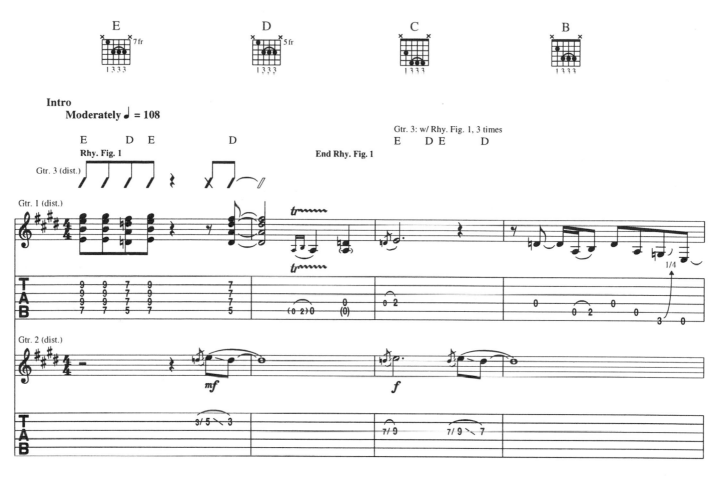

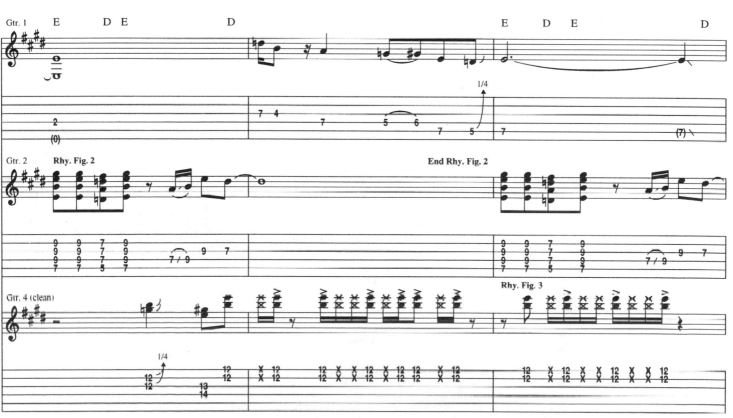

134

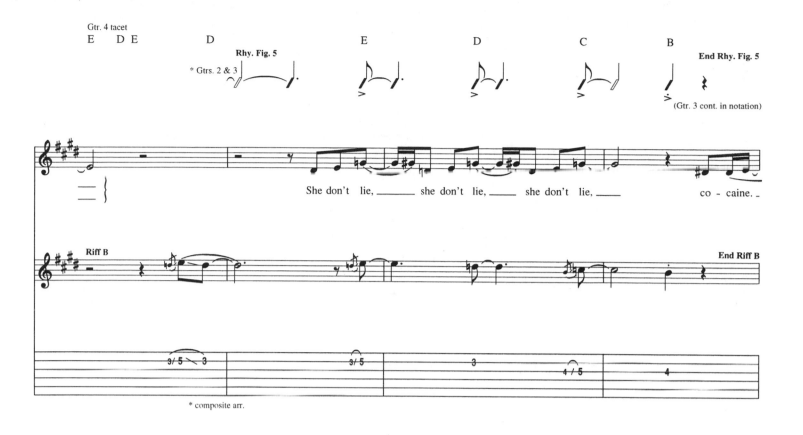

She don't lie, ____ she don't lie, ____ she don't lie, ____ co - caine. ____

* composite arr.

2. If you

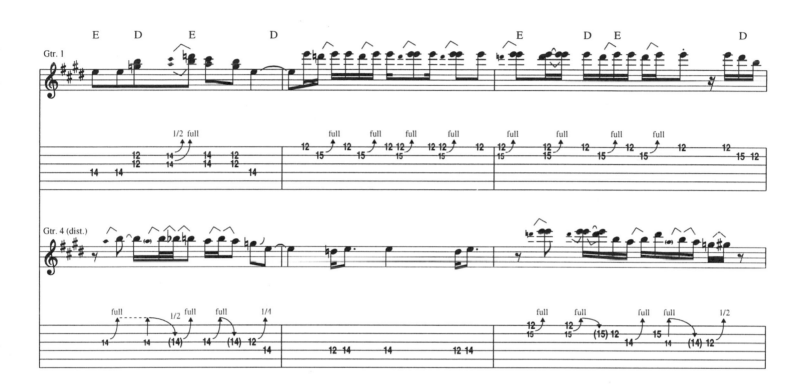

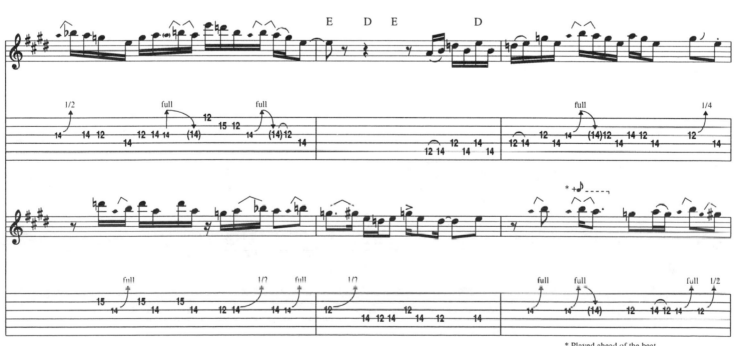

* Played ahead of the beat.

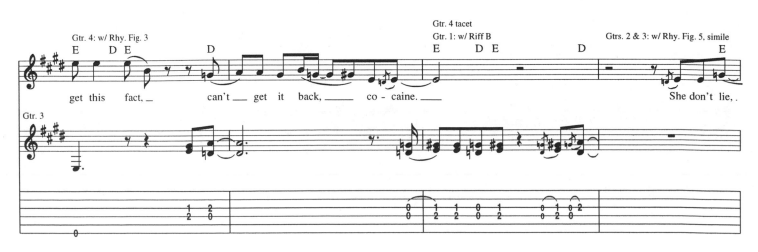

Outro

Gtrs. 2 & 3: w/ Rhy. Figs. 1 & 2, simile, till fade
Gtr. 4: w/ Rhy. Fig. 7, simile, till fade

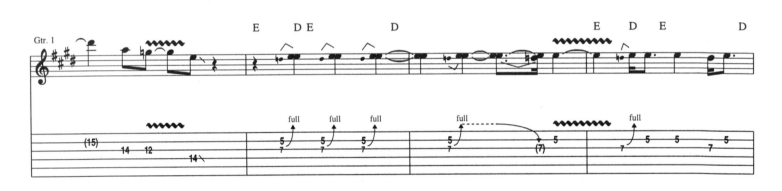

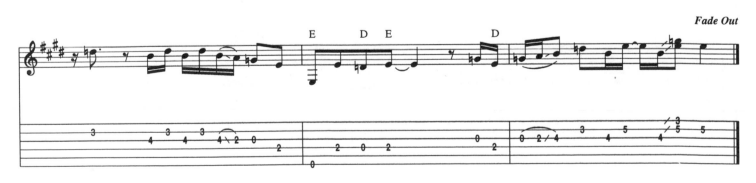

140

Wonderful Tonight

Words and Music by Eric Clapton

And then she asks ___ me, "Do I look al - right?"_ And I say,
And then she asks ___ me, "Do ya feel al - right?"_ And I say,
And then I tell ___ her, as I turn out the light, ___ I say, "My

"Yes, you _ look won-der - ful ___ to - night."_
"Yes, I ___ feel won-der - ful ___ to - night."_
darlin', you _ are won-der - ful ___ to - night."_

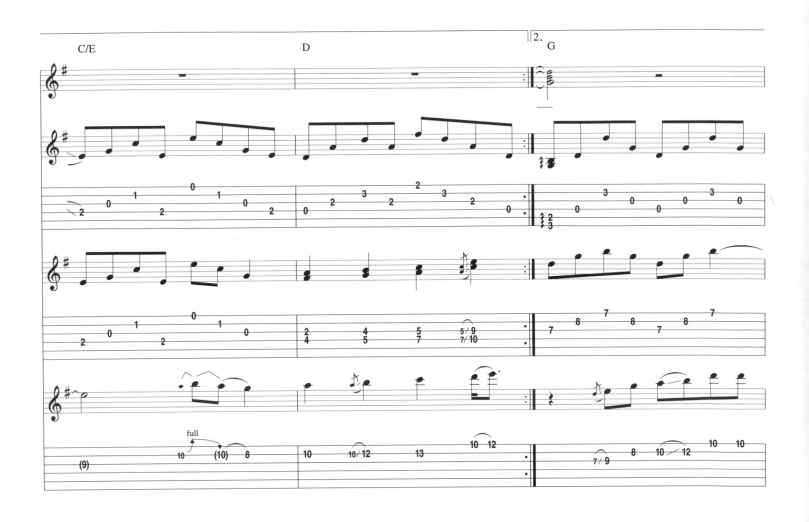

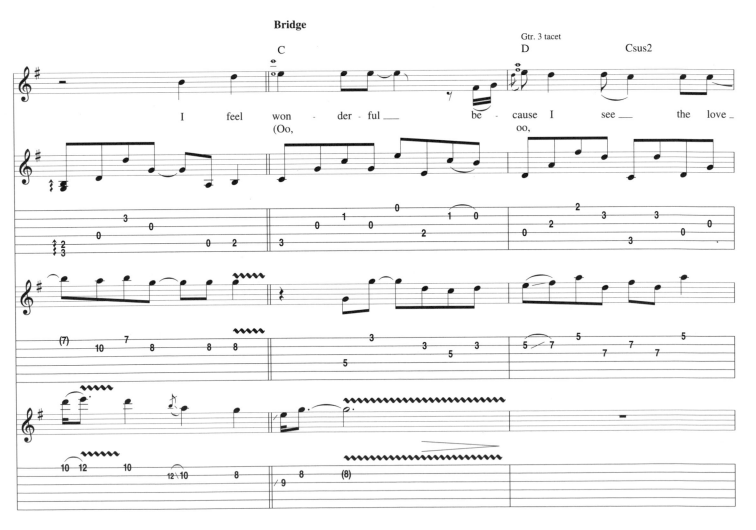

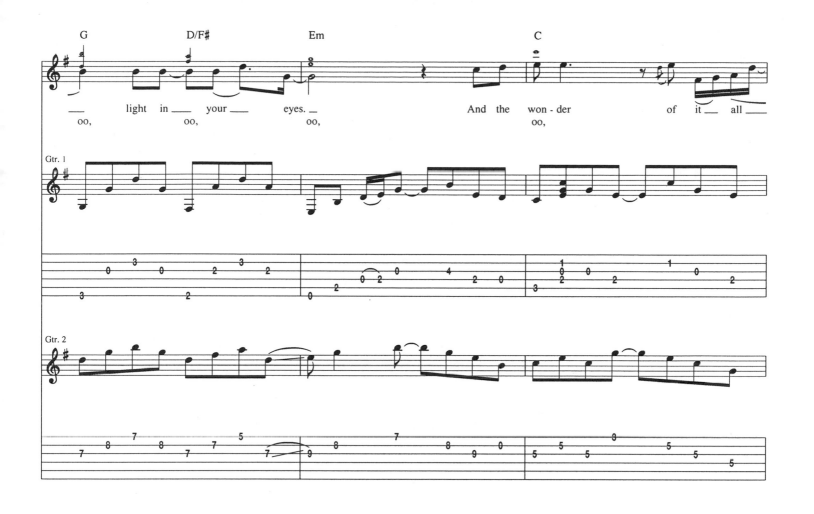

light in ___ your ___ eyes. ___   And the won - der   of it ___ all ___
oo,   oo,   oo,   oo,

___   is that you   just   don't ___ re - al - ize ___ how ___ much ___ I love ___
oo,   oo,   oo.)

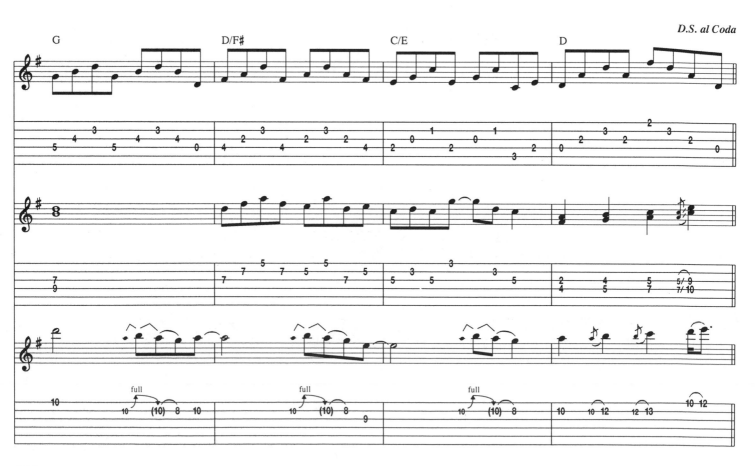

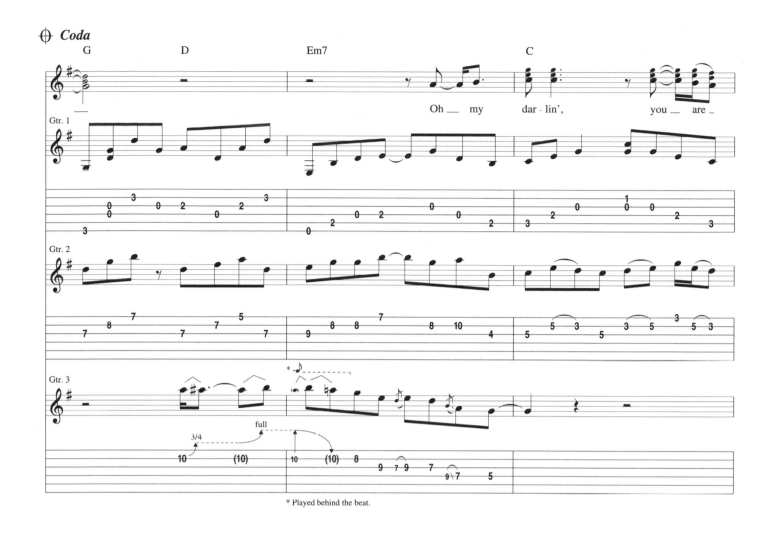

Promises

Words and Music by Richard Feldman and Roger Linn

keep on row - ing a - way ___ on a dis - tant sea, ___ 'cause I don't ___
Hav - in' lov - ers and friends ___ is all ___ good and fine, ___ but I don't ___

love you ___ and you don't ___ love me.
like yours ___ and you don't ___ like

2. You

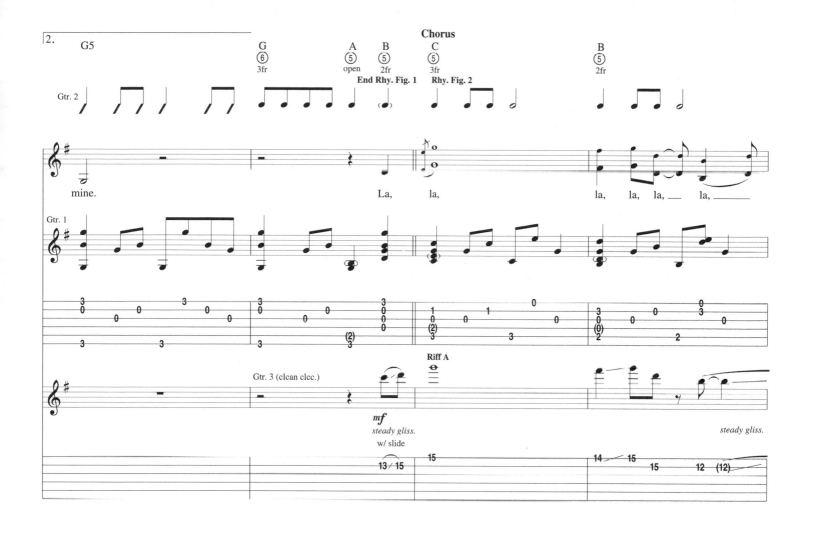

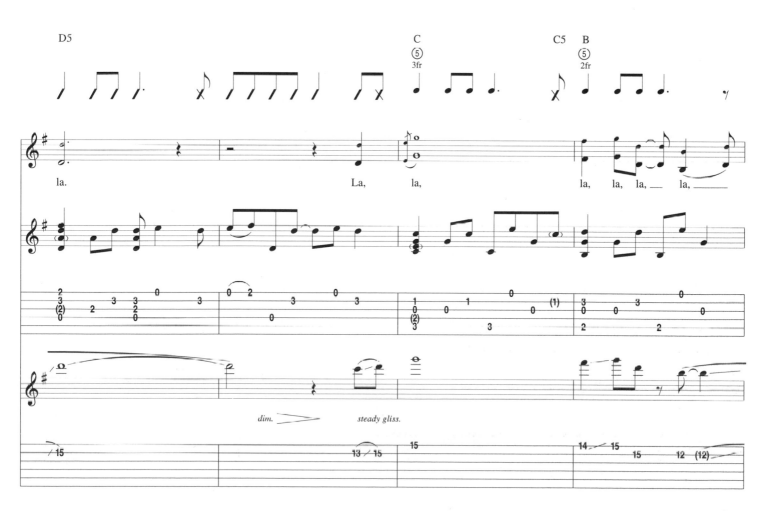

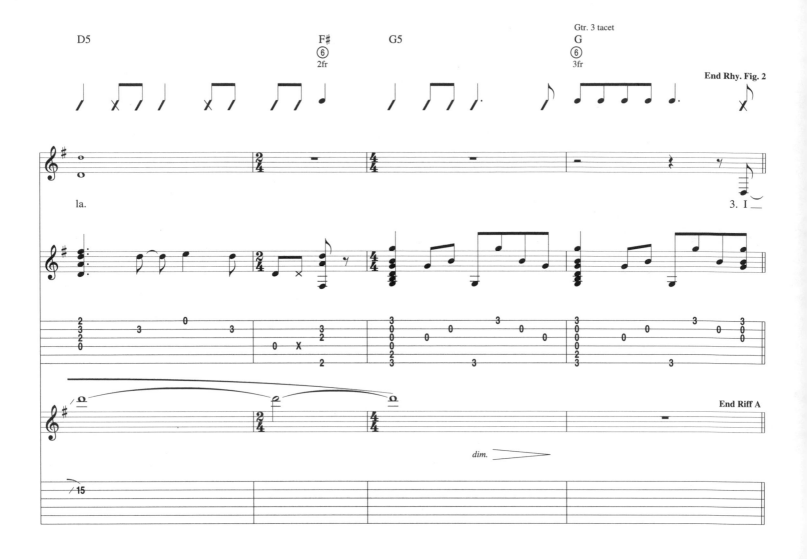

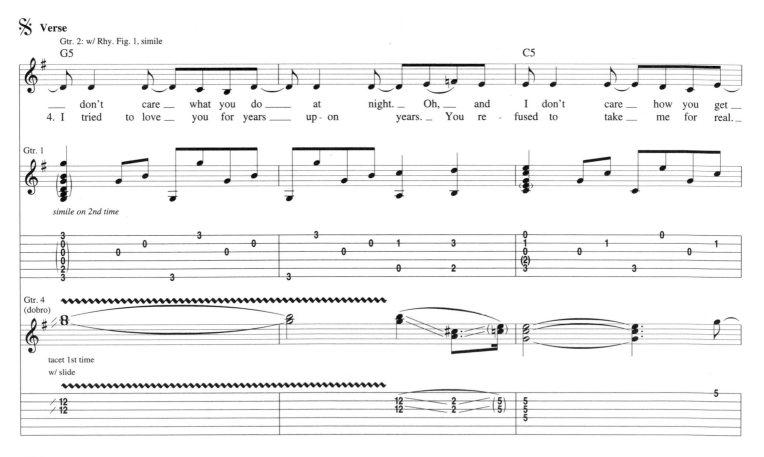

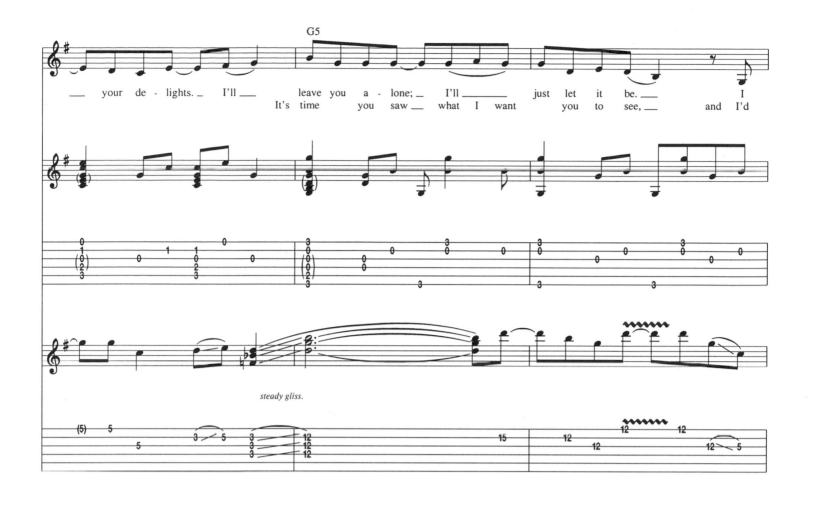

your de - lights.__ I'll __ leave you a - lone; I'll _____ just let it be.__ I
It's time you saw __ what I want you to see, __ and I'd

steady gliss.

don't love you and you don't ____ love me.
still love you if you'd just ____ love me.

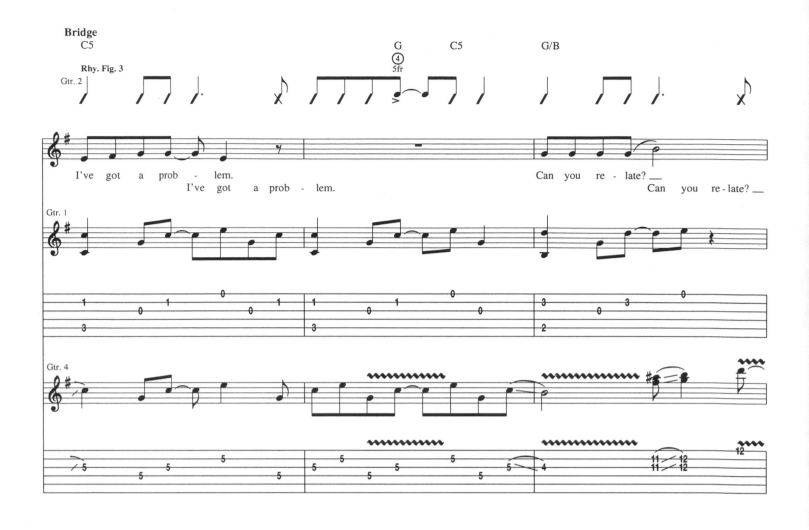
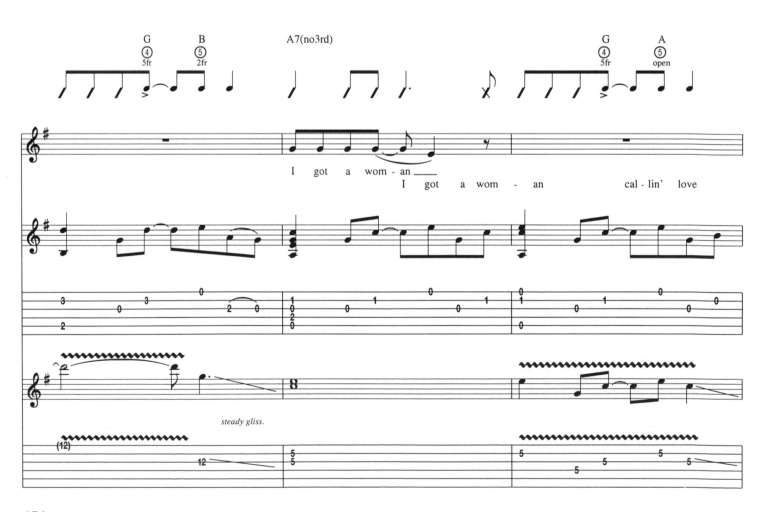

* position halfway between 3rd & 4th fret

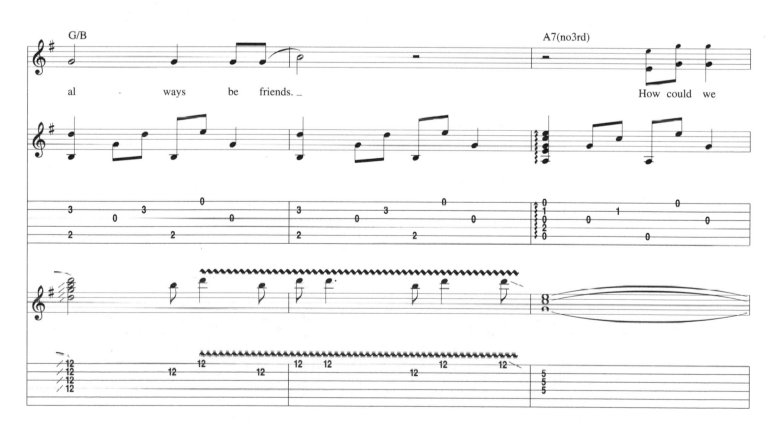

Gtr. 4: w/ Fill 1, 2nd time

* play 1st time

Chorus

Gtr. 2: w/ Rhy Fig. 2, simile, 1st time
Gtr. 2: w/ Rhy Fig. 2, 1st 7 meas., simile, 2nd time
Gtr. 3: w/ Riff A, 1st time
Gtr. 3: w/ Riff A, 1st 7 meas., 2nd time

Gtr. 4: w/ Fill 2, 2nd time

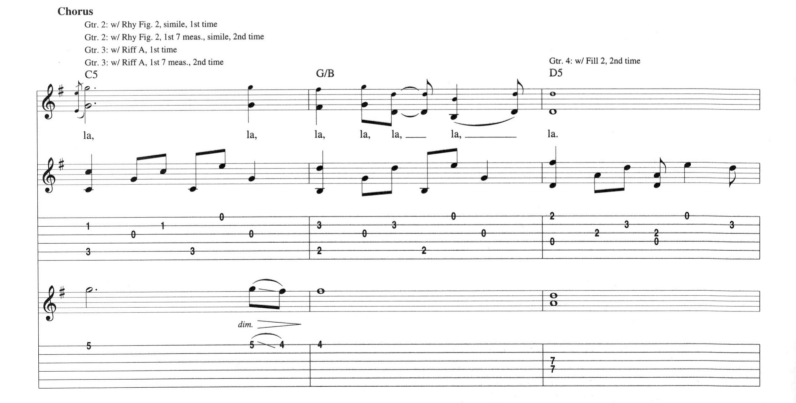

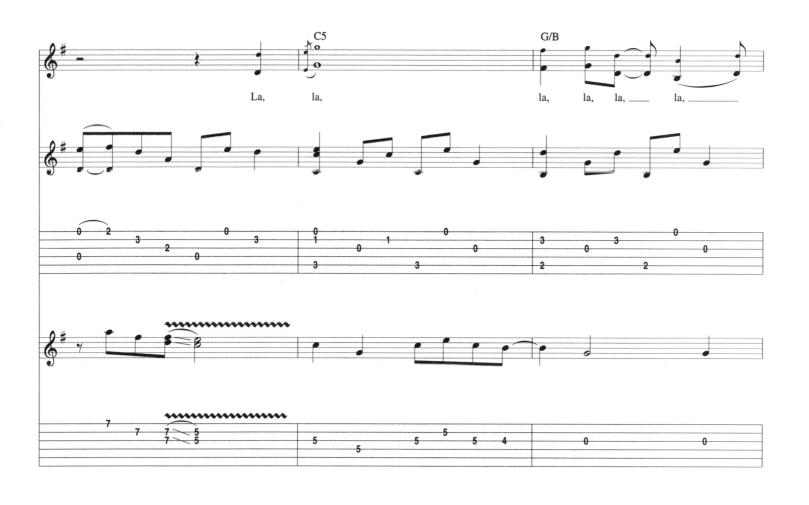

Gtr. 4: w/ Fill 3, 2nd time (see next page)

To Coda ⊕

D.S. al Coda

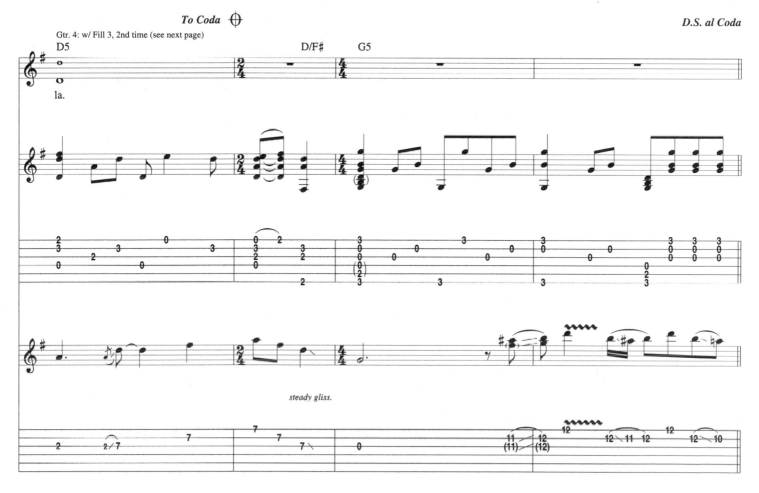

steady gliss.

 *Coda*

Outro
Gtr. 2: w/ Rhy. Fig. 2, 1st 4 meas., simile
Gtr. 3: w/ Riff A, 1st 4 meas.

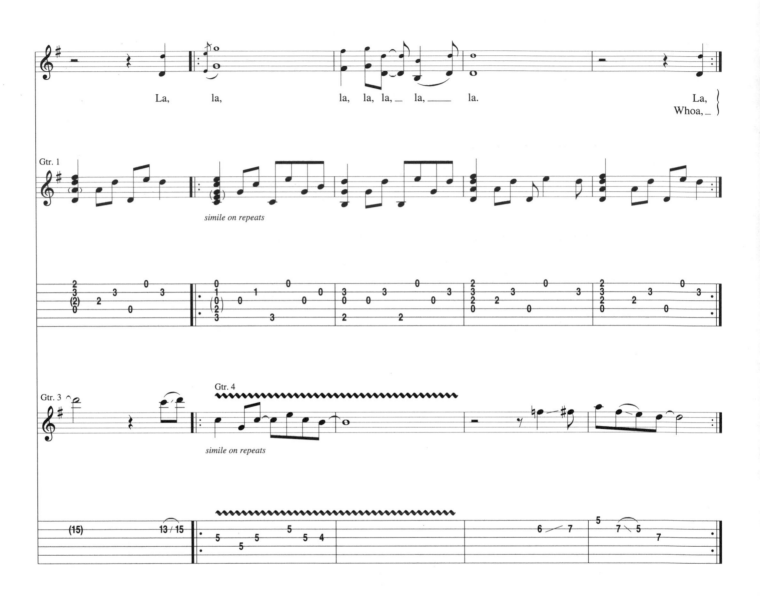

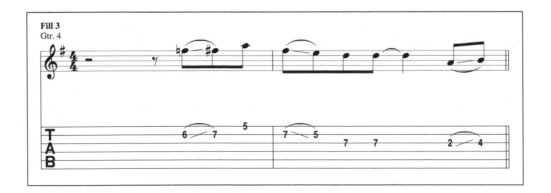

I Can't Stand It

Words and Music by Eric Clapton

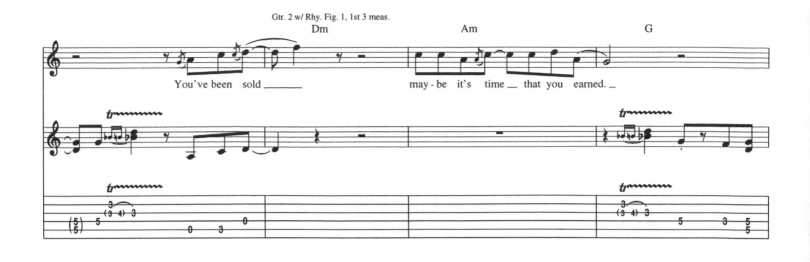

Chorus

Gtrs. 1 & 2: w/ Rhy. Figs. 3 & 3A

Gtr. 3 tacet

I can't stand ___ it. You're run-ning a-round; ___ I can't stand ___

___ it. You're fool-in' a - round; ___ I can't stand ___ it. You're play-in' a - round with my heart. ___

Verse

Gtr. 3: w/ Fill 1 (see next page)

Gtr. 2: w/ Rhy. Fig. 4, simile

Gtr. 3 tacet

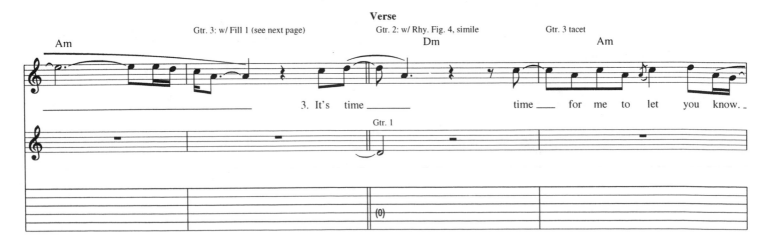

3. It's time _____ time ___ for me to let you know.

Gtr. 1

Ain't no crime, _____ no crime to let your feel - ings show._

Chorus

Gtrs. 1 & 2: w/ Rhy. Figs. 3 & 3A, 1st 6 meas., simile

I can't stand _ it. You're fun-nin' a - round;_ I can't stand_

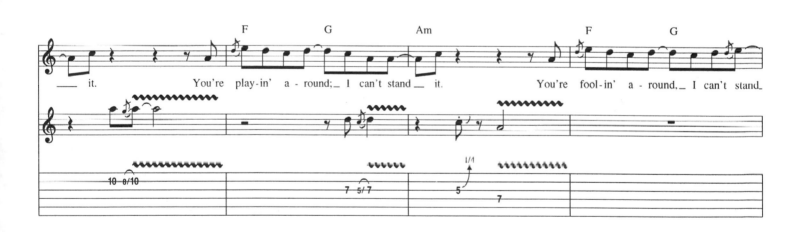

_ it. You're play-in' a - round;_ I can't stand _ it. You're fool-in' a - round,_ I can't stand_

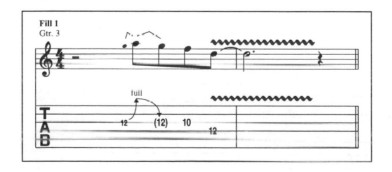

Guitar Notation Legend

Guitar Music can be notated three different ways: on a *musical staff*, in *tablature*, and in *rhythm slashes*.

RHYTHM SLASHES are written above the staff. Strum chords in the rhythm indicated. Use the chord diagrams found at the top of the first page of the transcription for the appropriate chord voicings. Round noteheads indicate single notes.

THE MUSICAL STAFF shows pitches and rhythms and is divided by bar lines into measures. Pitches are named after the first seven letters of the alphabet.

TABLATURE graphically represents the guitar fingerboard. Each horizontal line represents a string, and each number represents a fret.

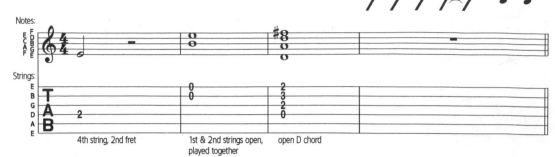

4th string, 2nd fret | 1st & 2nd strings open, played together | open D chord

HALF-STEP BEND: Strike the note and bend up 1/2 step.

WHOLE-STEP BEND: Strike the note and bend up one step.

GRACE NOTE BEND: Strike the note and bend up as indicated. The first note does not take up any time.

SLIGHT (MICROTONE) BEND: Strike the note and bend up 1/4 step.

BEND AND RELEASE: Strike the note and bend up as indicated, then release back to the original note. Only the first note is struck.

PRE-BEND: Bend the note as indicated, then strike it.

VIBRATO: The string is vibrated by rapidly bending and releasing the note with the fretting hand.

WIDE VIBRATO: The pitch is varied to a greater degree by vibrating with the fretting hand.

HAMMER-ON: Strike the first (lower) note with one finger, then sound the higher note (on the same string) with another finger by fretting it without picking.

PULL-OFF: Place both fingers on the notes to be sounded. Strike the first note and without picking, pull the finger off to sound the second (lower) note.

LEGATO SLIDE: Strike the first note and then slide the same fret-hand finger up or down to the second note. The second note is not struck.

SHIFT SLIDE: Same as legato slide, except the second note is struck.

TRILL: Very rapidly alternate between the notes indicated by continuously hammering on and pulling off.

TAPPING: Hammer ("tap") the fret indicated with the pick-hand index or middle finger and pull off to the note fretted by the fret hand.

NATURAL HARMONIC: Strike the note while the fret-hand lightly touches the string directly over the fret indicated.

PINCH HARMONIC: The note is fretted normally and a harmonic is produced by adding the edge of the thumb or the tip of the index finger of the pick hand to the normal pick attack.

PICK SCRAPE: The edge of the pick is rubbed down (or up) the string, producing a scratchy sound.

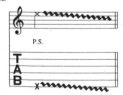

MUFFLED STRINGS: A percussive sound is produced by laying the fret hand across the string(s) without depressing, and striking them with the pick hand.

PALM MUTING: The note is partially muted by the pick hand lightly touching the string(s) just before the bridge.

RAKE: Drag the pick across the strings indicated with a single motion.

TREMOLO PICKING: The note is picked as rapidly and continuously as possible.

VIBRATO BAR DIVE AND RETURN: The pitch of the note or chord is dropped a specified number of steps (in rhythm) then returned to the original pitch.

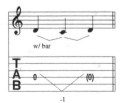

VIBRATO BAR SCOOP: Depress the bar just before striking the note, then quickly release the bar.

VIBRATO BAR DIP: Strike the note and then immediately drop a specified number of steps, then release back to the original pitch.